YOUR
IN 1996

AQUARIUS

YOUR LIFE
IN 1990

AQUARIUS

January 21 to February 18

ROGER ELLIOT

Futura

A Futura Book

First published in Great Britain in 1989
by Futura Publications, a Division of
Macdonald & Co (Publishers) Ltd
London & Sydney

ISBN 0 7088 4269 0

Photoset in North Wales by
Derek Doyle and Associates, Mold, Clwyd,
from computer discs prepared by the author.
Printed and bound in Great Britain by
Hazell, Watson & Viney Limited
Member of BPCC Limited
Aylesbury, Bucks

Futura Publications
A Division of
Macdonald & Co (Publishers) Ltd
66-73 Shoe Lane
London EC4P 4AB

A member of Maxwell Pergamon Publishing Corporation plc

Contents

ROGER ELLIOT is one of the top astrologers in the world today. As a writer, TV performer, teacher and consultant to many individuals, he spans the full range of astrology from scientific research to newspaper columns.

He provides a comprehensive astrology telephone service in Britain called *Ask the Oracle*, which is also available in Australia and Hong Kong.

Roger, born on June 25 under the sign of Cancer, lives in a Somerset manor house with his blonde Leo wife Suzie, and two teenage children Stephanie (Aries) and Mark (Aquarius) – not forgetting the Sagittarian Jack Russell terrier Sebastian.

For information about Roger Elliot's Starlife astrology service, please write to Starlife, Cossington, Somerset TA7 8JR.

My World
of Astrology

Welcome once again to my annual series of Zodiac books –
this time for the start of the new decade, 1990 – and greetings
to all my readers throughout the world.

It's a pleasure to indicate to you how the year ahead is likely
to unfold. I think you have plenty to look forward to, although
there are bound to be some setbacks and disappointments.

Remember that the daily forecasts are written in two sec-
tions. The first half, *written in italic*, refers to the whole world
and everyone in it. They give you an idea how other people are
likely to behave on the day in question – indeed, they may give
a clue to the national and international events taking place.

The second half of each daily forecast refers, as usual, to
yourself – as a birth-child of Aquarius – and the moods, events
and circumstances that may occur in your individual life. Sometimes they match the generalised forecast, but sometimes they
differ, simply because the planets that day are making a special
pattern as far as your Zodiac sign is concerned.

Once again I've included Wise Words at the end of each
monthly group of predictions. Most of them are wry or
funny, so don't take them all that seriously, but each of them
does refer, however obliquely, to the mood of the month.

As before, the section Mixing with Others enables you to
see how you relate to each of the twelve Zodiac signs.
Perhaps it will help you to understand personal links more
clearly, whether it's a friendship, a sexual partnership, a
relative or business contact.

Astrology of this kind is a team effort, a combination of
my expertise and your experience. Over the years I have
developed a complex array of skills for examining the
heavens. Using computers with vast memories, I can analyse
the planetary movements with considerable finesse.

Modern astrology is akin to weather forecasting. Today's
meteorologists use computers to compare wind and
temperature patterns now with all the patterns of yesteryear.
As a result, their forecasts are becoming more accurate. In

just the same way, I do not simply use theory.

From my own observations, as well as your thousands of letters over the years, I have been able to compare the evidence of the stars with actual reality. Every time you tell me that, yes – on such and such a date you did indeed have a headache, or no – in that particular month you did not start a new job, it goes into the computer. (Please don't worry – everything is completely confidential between you and me.)

But your evidence, private though it is, becomes part of my public store of knowledge; and this year, more than ever, my 1990 predictions are based as much on your experiences in the past as on my intuition in reading the stars.

So keep on writing to me. I love hearing your news and finding out whether my predictions are true. The more feedback I get from you, the more accurate I can be.

The reason is, you see, that patterns in the sky repeat themselves, just as weather patterns do. Every time Venus forms an opposition to Saturn, say, there should be a similar kind of event in your life.

Obviously the precise circumstances will vary from one Aquarius to the next. A teenager, unemployed in York, will experience the influence somewhat differently from a middle-aged businessman in New York. So you must always use common sense in interpreting my forecasts. Apply those words that are applicable. Ignore the remarks that clearly have no reference to your life.

Let me give you a fascinating example from my own life. A year or two ago, I suffered a heart attack – a small one, luckily, but still serious. As I recovered in hospital, I examined the planets to find out the astrological reason for this. Sure enough, I found that three planets – Mars, Saturn and Uranus – were exactly opposite the Sun in my horoscope, and square my Saturn: a clear indication of surprise, shock and bad news.

This planetary combination is rare but not unique, so I was interested to see when, in the past, the same planets made a similar impact on my horoscope. I found that in the fourth week of March 1981 both Mars and Saturn in the sky were exactly opposite my Saturn and square my Sun, while Uranus was exactly four signs away.

And what happened that week? My house burned down!

This stunning example that astrology really works raises some interesting points. I did not 'cause' either event; they were acts of fate that happened to me. Does that mean that the next time this planetary configuration occurs – in 1996 – I must willy-nilly put up with whatever fate hurls at me?

Or can I mitigate its effect? I believe I can – and should. Astrology gives clear warning of the happiness or sadness in store for us, but it's up to us to cool these influences, or encourage them, depending on what we want. I have learnt from my mistake. I knew, after all, about this impending 'heart-attack' warning, but had simply assumed that it would be a hard-working time. Because I did not cool the influence down – through relaxation and stress control – fate did it for me!

So bear this in mind as you read my forecasts for you. The real effect of the stars on your life may, in the end, be unavoidable; but you can still control how to respond.

I've tried my best in this book to give you fair warning of the influences ahead. But do remember that I'm always willing to help with your personal problems. If you want to learn more about astrology, and get your own horoscope in some way, write to me at Starlife, Cossington, Somerset TA7 8JR. Wherever you live, whatever your difficulties, your letter will reach me.

In the meantime, the world rolls round. With so much space travel nowadays, it's easy to visualise our little globe, a gleam of blue and white in a black universe, apparently the only sign of life amid an empty deadness. But it isn't really like that. We are surrounded by invisible forces, most of them wanting to nurture life and goodness on this planet.

Of course there is pain, sadness and death. But the life-force is inexorable. Touch the source of that energy, and you will be filled with a sense of joy and well-being and purpose.

May this Aquarius book help you to widen your perspective and bring you closer to the source of all life.

God bless you, my friend.

ROGER ELLIOT

9

Technical
Note

Some people think that astrology is all psychic intuition, but it's a good deal more scientific than that.

First of all, using my computers, I prepare an *ephemeris* for 1990 listing the positions of the Sun and planets, together with all their midpoints, for each day of the year. They are grouped along a great circle in the sky called the *ecliptic* or Zodiac, which is divided into the twelve signs.

Then I prepare a daily *aspectarian* telling which planets are in line with each other, or in opposition, or square to each other, or whatever it may be. Let's take my own birthday as an example. On June 25 Mars is square Jupiter, while Mercury is quincunx Saturn. These are just two of fourteen aspects in force that day.

Now each planet represents a different quality in life. Mars stands for energy and enterprise, while Jupiter stands for happiness. So it's a broadly pleasant day, but the Mercury-Saturn contact means there will be some aggravation and arguments and disappointment.

That's why my general prediction for this day, as you can see on page 65 is *Quite a happy time, though there's a note of bullying in the air.* In fact, this combination could produce an international squabble.

The individual forecast that follows is based on a careful analysis of what these planets mean for Aquarius. Sometimes I am very scientific, noting the rulerships of the planets as far as you are concerned, and sometimes I simply get a mental picture of the various conflicting forces and imagine how a person like yourself would respond.

So it's a mixture of science and imagination – I hope! At all events, I trust it will be helpful to you.

If you ever need a technical description of your own horoscope, looking at all the planets, write to me at the address on the previous page.

Mixing
with Others

You may think that just because you're a Aquarius person you have got nothing in common with other Zodiac signs.

But in fact the twelve signs have a lot in common, because all the Zodiac signs are linked by an enthralling system of Elements and Modes. By discovering which Mode and Element you belong to, you can find out what you have in common with other signs – and what you don't!

Each sign belongs to one Mode and one Element. Naturally you get on well with other signs that share these qualities.

The Modes

Aries, Cancer, Libra and Capricorn belong to the **Cardinal Mode**. All the Cardinal signs are concerned with activity. In their differing ways they like to get things moving; to take practical steps; to start a new enterprise. So they resemble the cardinal points of the compass – north, south, east and west – in the sense that they point in a new direction.

Taurus, Leo, Scorpio and Aquarius all belong to the **Fixed Mode**. Fixed signs are exactly what they say they are: immovable and fixed, gaining strength from maintaining a situation rather than changing it. They have the virtue of persistence and the drawback of stubbornness.

If the Cardinal signs can be symbolised by a pointing finger, Fixed signs are represented by a clenched fist.

Gemini, Virgo, Sagittarius and Pisces belong to the **Mutable Mode**. Mutable signs express changeability. They are also called dualistic signs because their energy seems to fluctuate.

If Cardinal signs drive straight down the road, Mutable ones veer from side to side. This provides great flexibility of outlook, but also great unreliability and lack of constancy. Images like a flickering candle capture the basic Mutable quality.

11

The Elements

Capricorn, Taurus and Virgo belong to the **Earth** Element. Earth signs are solid, reliable and stable. The world tends to approve of earthy people, although they can be rather crude and indelicate at times. We like their common sense.

The drawback of these signs is their lack of enterprise and vision. They can become encased in materialism, and gradually action can become clogged by inertia.

Aries, Leo and Sagittarius belong to the **Fire** Element. All the Fire signs have a magical quality, enabling them to fire other people into activity. At their most creative, these signs have constant access to real enthusiasm. They are powered by an unending fuel store helping them to achieve a great deal. At their most destructive, however, the Fire signs use other people as fuel. They burn the energy out of them, leaving behind a trail of wrecked hearts.

Libra, Aquarius and Gemini belong to the **Air** Element. Air is an insubstantial Element. It breezes this way and that, carrying seeds from one part of the land to another. Traditionally it's linked with the transmission of ideas.

Air signs are communicative and sociable – bringing men and women together; spreading ideas and trying to change their surroundings. You can see the possible faults of these signs in the popular sayings 'too airy-fairy' or 'talking a lot of hot air'.

Cancer, Scorpio and Pisces belong to the **Water** Element. Water is the most mysterious of the four Elements. We are said to be born in the waters of the womb, or have evolved from earlier aquatic creatures, and spiritually we return to the great waters of eternity.

Water signs have a fine capacity to flow into the hearts and minds of other people. Like electricity through water, they are conducive to the ideas and feelings coming their way, and they respond very sensitively to their environment.

At worst, of course, they are wet, drippy and sloppy!

Aries
March 21 to April 20

Friendships Aries people like friends but hate to be dependent on them. They are self-reliant folk who, in the last resort, are quite happy on their own. They take friends at face value, and don't like people who are too moody or changeable or hanging back from making decisions. They enjoy the company of people who are enthusiastic, good-humoured and brave – just like themselves, in fact!

Sex Aries people are sexy, but that doesn't make them all Don Juans or nymphomaniacs. They have a strong, muscular sex nature that likes to impose itself on others. If anything, their sexuality is stronger than their need for love. Certainly they are self-centred people, and can ignore their partners' feelings.

Marriage Aries folk are not settlers by nature, but more like nomads or hunters. There's more fun for them in making new conquests than sticking with the same old mate. On the other hand, they hate failure – and what they have, they hold. So they can make loyal, stable marriage partners. If the marriage does get stale, Aries is the one to put a stop to the agony.

Aries (March 21 to April 20) **and You**

This is a friendly, relaxed relationship. You both like freedom, so won't cramp each other's style.

An **Aries friend** is a lot more energetic and open-minded than you, but you can still enjoy each other's company. 1990 rating: amusing and genuinely warm.

With an **Aries parent** you have a wonderful example of energy and high spirits. Hopefully you were always given freedom to do what you want. 1990 rating: good links.

If you have an **Aries child** you have a youngster who knows his own mind. Keep things light and optimistic. He is much more competitive than you. 1990 rating: you may agree to differ.

An **Aries boy-friend** lacks finesse, and enjoys a hard kind of love-making whereas you like a softer, more subtle approach. 1990 rating: poor at first, getting better.

An **Aries girl-friend** expects lively and forceful lovemaking. She wants you to be a real man – which isn't quite your style. 1990 rating: quite intense.

An **Aries husband** is not really the settling-down type. But then, neither are you. Added to which, you're a feminist and he isn't. 1990 rating: pressure from the rest of the family.

An **Aries wife** isn't your average housewife, but she shares your independence of outlook. So in the end you suit each other. 1990 rating: supportive in times of trouble, but indifferent to success.

An **Aries boss** is brisk, no-nonsense and practical. I think he respects you more than you think. A good business mixture. 1990 rating: perfectly nice, but you both want it to be a businesslike relationship, nothing more.

Taurus
April 21 to May 21

Friendship Taurean people are among the most gregarious folk in the Zodiac. They love being surrounded by friends, and seek to form firm, solid friendships that last forever. It's part of the deep Taurean need for security. But there's a generous side to the bargain as well. They love plying their friends with food and drink, making them feel at home.

Sex Taurus is one of the sexiest of Zodiac signs. There is a basic earthiness about their approach to sex. They love living in their own bodies and, through kissing and touching, making contact with a loved one's body. They are highly sensual, and the danger is they'll make sex the be-all and end-all of their relationships. If the body loses appeal, they lose interest. A Taurean can too often take the partner's feelings for granted.

14

Marriage Taureans are made for marriage. It's the most natural way for them to live, sharing with another and building up a strong, mutually supportive family. Ideally they are monogamist by nature, and want to stay faithful. They feel secure within marriage, and would only stray for sexual gratification. Otherwise they make loyal spouses.

Taurus (April 21 to May 21) and You

Quite a stubborn partnership. You can build a business or family, but with some heartbreak involved.

A **Taurus friend** will try to take quiet control of your life, but in the nicest possible way. This friend is very possessive, so you may try to escape. 1990 rating: respectful.

A **Taurus parent** will be generous one moment, a bit uptight the next. Your sweetness and light will make things easier. 1990 rating: you go your separate ways.

A **Taurus child** is a stolid youngster who is a good deal more conventional than you. Practical but a little slow in thinking. 1990 rating: extra attention needed.

A **Taurus boy-friend** brings things nicely down to the physical. But you are a good deal more high-minded, and don't like the gross side of life. 1990 rating: he's thinking of other things.

A **Taurus girl-friend** is a cuddly woman who's very possessive. She may swallow you up with love. Pride can get in the way of common sense. 1990 rating: she's keener on you than you think.

A **Taurus husband** is willing to do some of the housework that you get bored with. A good solid breadwinner, and a fine family man. 1990 rating: he's worried about his career.

A **Taurus wife** is attractive in your eyes. She's a real earth goddess type. She can act as an anchor in your emotional life. 1990 rating: pride gets in the way of happiness.

With a **Taurus boss** you can have an efficient and useful relationship. You make a good partnership, especially if you are equal partners. 1990 rating: leisurely time, so you'll get to know each other better.

15

Gemini
May 22 to June 21

Friendship Geminians are the most friendly people in the Zodiac, though, to be honest, they are better at making casual acquaintances than deep personal ties. One reason is that people find them an attractive type, easy to be with, because they have the gift of adapting themselves to suit the company. But they are fair-weather friends. If trouble looms, they don't want to know.

Sex Gemini people talk themselves into and out of love, almost as though it were a game. Gemini is not a highly-sexed sign, even though they may have plenty of sexual experience. Instead, sex for them is a rather special form of conversation. It does not necessarily involve them in deep feelings. But it's quite possible for Geminians to enjoy non-sexual relationships.

Marriage As Gemini is the most devious, two-faced and freewheeling of all Zodiac signs, it follows that marriage is not really suited to their nature. But they can still make a success of marriage. They need a partner who can keep them on their toes; who can spring surprises; who is more a lover than a spouse; and who, if necessary, can turn a blind eye every time they stray.

Gemini (May 22 to June 21) and You

A wonderful partnership, so long as you stick with each other. Lots of intellectual companionship.

A **Gemini friend** is quick to become friends. Together you can have some wonderful times – very fast-witted and good-humoured. 1990 rating: enjoyable.

If you have a **Gemini parent** you will have had a lively, good-humoured relationship. You suit each other, and should still like each other. 1990 rating: you see more in each other as the years pass.

A **Gemini child** has tantrums at times. He's a restless youngster with a wide variety of interests. Good mental links between you. 1990 rating: you're very proud of each other, really.

A **Gemini boy-friend** can have a super affair with you, but it's rather here today and gone tomorrow. Friendly rather than sexy, actually. 1990 rating: marvellous at first.

A **Gemini girl-friend** is inventive and jolly, but a bit nervous at times. It's a quick, lively, rather insubstantial relationship. 1990 rating: perfectly friendly, but you're held back.

A **Gemini husband** suits you well, so long as life goes with a swing. Neither of you is terribly good at dealing with crises. 1990 rating: don't push your luck.

A **Gemini wife** is a marvellous pal, and a good partner to you. She's happy to be your equal in life. 1990 rating: time for a second honeymoon.

If you have a **Gemini boss** he may not tell you everything you should know. He's a lively chap, not really reliable, and you make a good partnership. 1990 rating: you mean a lot to each other, underneath the badinage.

Cancer
June 22 to July 22

Friendship Cancerians are clannish people at the best of times. They want to be friendly, but they can't help being suspicious of strangers at first. Once they've decided to make someone a friend, they tend to adopt them completely, drawing them into the family, so to speak. Cancerians have a great ability to identify with their friends' feelings, and love sharing.

Sex Although shy at first, Cancer folk soon fall hook, line and sinker for the right sweetheart. They're terrible clingers, hanging on for dear life if a lover seems to be losing interest. Sexually they have access to deep, ecstatic feelings. Physical pleasure is nothing compared with the spiritual orgasms they are capable of experiencing.

Marriage Cancerians are born to be married. They want to share their life with the perfect partner. Cancer men have a good deal of tenderness in their natures; they like strong-minded women who will look after them – indeed, mother them. Cancer women are very feminine, and need men who are kind, loyal and humorous – in short, a homely chap.

Cancer (June 22 to July 22) and You

Not an ideal mixture, but you can learn to live together. Cancer is too moody and touchy for your liking.

A **Cancer friend** can get moody, which you don't like. You are too frank and honest at times. Otherwise it's a happy relationship. 1990 rating: an energetic time together.

With a **Cancer parent** there are likely to be differences of opinion and outlook. You are modern, whereas Cancer is traditional-minded. 1990 rating: new surroundings.

Towards a **Cancer child** you must be patient. Don't force your attitudes on him. He needs lots of mothering, until he starts rebelling! 1990 rating: find a way of avoiding trouble.

A **Cancer boy-friend** is always looking for the ideal wife and mother, so he'll try to tie you down to marriage. 1990 rating: you're a bit straight-laced for him.

A **Cancer girl-friend** brings lots of warm, possessive emotions into her love-making. She may make you feel a bit cold and aloof. 1990 rating: a steady year – perhaps leading to marriage.

A **Cancer husband** is happy to wash up, look after the children and help you out around the home – but he's also a moody, difficult man at times. 1990 rating: happy changes.

A **Cancer wife** will be over-emotional at times, but she's a good balance to your over-rational approach to life. 1990 rating: apparently a steady year – with tensions underneath.

If you have a **Cancer boss** there will be a coolly friendly working relationship. You contribute different talents, but won't always see eye to eye. 1990 rating: an unsuitable liaison.

Leo
July 23 to August 23

Friendship All Leo folk thrive on friendship, but Leo likes to be the dominant partner. They want to be flattered, praised, loved and enjoyed – that's what friendship means to them. But that isn't all. For a Leo, the heart will always rule the head. They would do anything for a friend – indeed, they put friendship above all.

Sex There's only one thing to do on a hot afternoon – and that is to make love! So think Leo people, anyway. Nothing pleases them more than someone of the opposite sex making eyes at them. They love to be wooed. Falling in love comes very naturally to Leo folk. It's probably true to say that a Leo can't feel truly fulfilled without a good sex life.

Marriage Leos may enjoy flirting at parties, but in the end they are looking for a steady marriage. They need courtship and security at the same time. If ever a marriage breaks up, it can shatter the Leo heart – and like a broken mirror it never quite recovers. A Leo man needs a warmly responsive wife, while the Leo woman wants fidelity and affection.

Leo (July 23 to August 23) **and You**

This is a lively, idealistic pairing.
You can truly enjoy each other's company.

A **Leo friend** is a good, loyal friend. He will stand by you, inspire you and give lots of encouragement. 1990 rating: time to help a charity together.

If you have a **Leo parent** there will be minor clashes but on the whole the rapport is warmly friendly. You may be more intelligent. 1990 rating: excellent – truly compatible for once!

With a **Leo child** you must flatter and cajole, but not let it go to his head. He's a headstrong youngster. 1990 rating: amiable.

A **Leo boy-friend** will woo you with flowers, chat and

laughter. A real holiday romance – perhaps a bit too good to be true? 1990 rating: be more cynical about this relationship.

A **Leo girl-friend** is a warm, fun-loving woman who does want to be treated as a lady. She'll find you a bit distant at times. 1990 rating: give it more time.

A **Leo husband** should be happy with you, though he will take the limelight at any social gathering. 1990 rating: you need more freedom.

A **Leo wife** forms a marvellous partnership with you, and you should be very happy together. Let's hope it's a lifelong love affair. 1990 rating: don't nag.

A **Leo boss** can be an inspiring figure. He likes to take the lead, but he does respect your mind, too. 1990 rating: some cheering news, but you may still part.

Virgo
August 24 to September 22

Friendship Virgo people distrust strangers. When they meet a new person, they're distant at first. Only when they feel safe will they relax and become more personal. Even then, they are not as friendly as most Zodiac signs. They don't mix as freely, and are much more choosy about friends. They like people who are kindly, intelligent and observant – like themselves.

Sex Traditionally Virgo is the least sexy of all the Zodiac. Virgo people are capable of strong platonic friendships, and they don't seem to need sex as much as other people. Perhaps they need awakening – and once they realise how exciting it can be, they enjoy a splendid sex life. Some Virgoans, particularly women, put themselves on a pedestal, pretending to be far too good for the opposite sex.

Marriage Virgoans tend to remain unmarried longer than other signs. They need space to themselves, where they can be private. Virgoan men need a strong-minded wife who won't be too domineering. He needs someone who will give him enthusiasm as well as encouragement. Virgoan women look for emotional security. They are the kind to have a career outside marriage.

Virgo (August 24 to September 22) **and You**

An intelligent, interesting combination. You get on well, but it's not a desperately warm relationship.

A **Virgo friend** may get bogged down in details and fall into criticising and nagging. Keep the friendship idealistic. 1990 rating: splendid. You have plenty in common this year.

If you have a **Virgo parent** there will be a reassuring haven if you get fretful and unhappy in your emotional life. A cool sort of upbringing. 1990 rating: lots to look forward to. You'll be making joint plans.

With a **Virgo child** you have a worrier on your hands. This child is intelligent, and needs a push to get ahead. 1990 rating: steadily on course. You're doing well.

A **Virgo boy-friend** is a bit dry and studious, and will make love in the same way. It's a cool, humorous and private romance. 1990 rating: enjoy him while you can. He may not be around for long – or is there a rival?

A **Virgo girl-friend** is a bright woman who suits you nicely. She won't make demands you can't meet. 1990 rating: surprisingly good – maybe even marriage. You'll certainly be making long-term plans.

A **Virgo husband** will make a legal, decent, honest woman of you – but is that what you want? Actually you suit each other pretty well. 1990 rating: he may get frisky. Give him a bit of freedom, and he won't stray far.

With a **Virgo wife** you make a tidy pair who are wrapped up in yourselves. Your children will tend to take after you. 1990 rating: getting better, so be patient.

A **Virgo boss** is a perfectionist. Treat him right, and he will be generous to you in return. 1990 rating: he's full of ideas, but few of them are good.

21

Libra
September 23 to October 23

Friendship Librans thrive on friendship – more than any other Zodiac sign. Without friends they feel lost, only half-alive, for they are so amicable themselves. They mix easily, but can quickly detect if someone is 'not nice'. They adore small talk, chats on the phone, and social gatherings of all kinds. They have the rare ability to stay in touch with childhood friends.

Sex Librans are made for loving! They are one of those Zodiac signs who do distinguish between sex and love. Love without sex is okay, but sex without love is abhorrent. In the right relationship, they want to share themselves, body and soul, with the person they love. They are the psychological type who is drawn to their opposite – not always a good thing!

Marriage Of all Zodiac signs, Libra is the one most suited to marriage. They seem to be born as 'twin souls', and spend their lives looking for the ideal mate. Librans of both sexes need someone who is a good pal as well as lover. Libran men need an organised woman who isn't bossy. Libran women feel they need a real macho man who will look after them forever.

Libra (September 23 to October 23) **and You**

This is one of the best Zodiac combinations. You have lots of affection for each other, and seem attractive to others.

A **Libra friend** is a good person but lacks drive. You'll be friends without getting really close. There won't be tension between you. 1990 rating: bright-eyed and bushy-tailed.

With a **Libra parent** you have a kindly and understanding person who will always wish you the best. Don't interfere too much in his or her life. 1990 rating: some rows.

If you have a **Libra child** there will be a lovely mental

rapport between you. This is a clever child who should do well. 1990 rating: intense at times.

A **Libra boy-friend** is a gentle lover who wants to bring out the best in you. So once you're hooked, you'll tend to stay together. 1990 rating: looks good, especially if you've just met.

A **Libra girl-friend** is an adorable creature, though she'll want you to take more of a male lead than you want to. 1990 rating: sexually exciting.

With a **Libra husband** you make a charming couple – kindly, intelligent, sociable. It's more a mental than physical link. You'll have interesting children. 1990 rating: you're maturing nicely.

A **Libra wife** is not a housewife but a lovely adornment. This is a good mixture for long-term happiness. 1990 rating: could be the point of no return.

With a **Libra boss** you have a fine relationship, especially if you work in a pleasant environment. You can be friends outside office hours, too. 1990 rating: trouble in the firm means you may split up.

Scorpio
October 24 to November 22

Friendship Scorpio people are highly suspicious of new-comers. They don't make friends easily, and they can test their friendships so severely that they frighten would-be pals away. But once a true friendship is formed, it lasts for life. As far as Scorpio is concerned, friendship is a matter of utter loyalty. Friendship with members of their own sex is very important.

Sex Sex is a deeper, richer experience for Scorpio than perhaps for anyone else. At the same time, they manage to make sex far more complex and meaningful than it need be. Many Scorpians are frightened of sexual power. Raw sex, without love, worries them more than most people. It's certainly hard for them to have a casual, lightweight affair. As in so many other aspects of their lives, it's all or nothing.

Marriage Scorpians don't take their marriage vows lightly. They mean to keep them, through bad times as well as good. They can be very jealous if slighted, but within a happy relationship they are the happiest of partners, for they are capable of much devotion. Scorpio men need a woman who can be a real soul-mate. Scorpio women need a strong man – the tougher the better.

Scorpio (October 24 to November 22) and You

Quite a tense relationship at times, because Scorpio loves secrets and you love telling the truth.

A **Scorpio friend** will try to dominate you. Don't get taken in by the Scorpio moods and emotional blackmail. 1990 rating: fretful this year.

With a **Scorpio parent** there are bound to be problems. You may prefer to say nothing rather than get into an argument. 1990 rating: you may feel you're being bossed around too much.

A **Scorpio child** is secretive, intense and possessive, while you are just the opposite. So there will have been differences in the past. 1990 rating: something to celebrate.

A **Scorpio boy-friend** has a tough streak in his love-making that you may like in theory but not in practice. 1990 rating: you may be one of several girl-friends.

A **Scorpio girl-friend** is passionate, once you've turned her on. You're more easy-going, so she'll feel you don't get involved enough. 1990 rating: great, if you can keep her.

A **Scorpio husband** is the strong, silent type. You are much more sociable and independent, and don't like his jealousy. 1990 rating: a new beginning.

A **Scorpio wife** is an intense woman who won't like you straying from home – a pity, as you enjoy your freedom. You can gradually grow apart. 1990 rating: both of you are changing and maturing.

A **Scorpio boss** is a hard taskmaster. He has passed through a difficult patch, but is much more positive and dynamic now. 1990 rating: quite nice on a day-to-day basis – but for ever?

Sagittarius
November 23 to December 21

Friendship Sagittarians are friendly – for a while – but people cannot rely on them. They can drop friends as easily as they can pick them up – without much heartbreak. Most Sagittarians have a built-in charm that never fails to attract. There's a relaxed, informal manner which doesn't really look for lasting links. They like new people, so old pals are taken for granted.

Sex They have a very flirtatious manner that enjoys chatting up the opposite sex. There's also an element of victory involved. They like to win hearts, and at times they get a thrill from leaving a broken heart by the wayside. Sagittarians enjoy sex on impulse, perhaps in exotic locations! They can get bored with the sameness of love-making with the same old partner!

Marriage Sagittarians are not the most monogamous of people. It's hard for them to maintain interest in one person all their lives. So they need partners who have the same variety-seeking outlook on life that Sagittarians have. Men born under Sagittarius appreciate a woman with a mind of her own. Sagittarian women respond to real men, full of zest for life.

Sagittarius (November 23 to December 21) **and You**

*An easy relationship, with few hang-ups
so long as you keep talking to each other.*

A **Sagittarius friend** has lovely wit and great strength of character. You couldn't pick a better pal. You have so many things in common. 1990 rating: eight out of ten.

A **Sagittarius parent** will have given you a bright and breezy upbringing. There should be relatively few problems between you. 1990 rating: not very close.

25

With a **Sagittarius child** there may be too much zest and vigour, and not enough patience and decorum. 1990 rating: surprisingly good.

A **Sagittarius boy-friend** is terrific fun. But because you are both independent-minded, it won't be an up-tight love affair. 1990 rating: a crunch-time in the relationship.

A **Sagittarius girl-friend** is a marvellous companion for you. If you try to control her too much, she'll evade your grasp. 1990 rating: give her encouragement, not criticism.

A **Sagittarius husband** is a lovely choice as partner. He'll keep you entertained, thrilled and laughing all your life. 1990 rating: better, but not good.

A **Sagittarius wife** gives you a super marriage – if you can make it last! Although you like each other, you like to look around for other companions. 1990 rating: this marriage needs more sparkle.

A **Sagittarius boss** can be reckless at times. Use your common sense to calm him down. Actually you get on well. 1990 rating: efficient, but not very warm in your personal relations.

Capricorn
December 22 to January 20

Friendship Capricorn folk make friends with difficulty – but once made, they tend to remain friends for life. The wall around the Capricorn heart makes it hard for us to get to know them well. Friendship for the Capricorn type is not a light-hearted, take-it-or-leave-it affair. It must be based on real virtues such as trust, honour and the readiness to help.

Sex Capricorn people have such a cold manner at times that they appear unsexy. Actually they are highly sexed, though it does not always flow out in a harmonious way. They are not flirty types. They adopt a serious approach to life, and can turn nasty and jealous if slighted. Yet their planet Saturn is linked to the old Roman orgies, so they can certainly let themselves go! They can turn from frost to warmth in a split second!

Marriage Marriage is a solemn matter to Capricorn folk. They intend to make it last for life. Once married, they feel they own their partners. They don't look for freedom or adventure. All their energies are devoted to maintaining the marriage as it is. This can lead to a stale situation where they take their spouses too much for granted.

Capricorn (December 22 to January 20) and You

An interesting, intelligent mix.
You'll find Capricorn a bit heavy going after a while.

A **Capricorn friend** knows his own mind. But you're a bit of a rebel, and will enjoy thinking your own thoughts. Good for business links. 1990 rating: could be a big row, leading to the end of the friendship.

A **Capricorn parent** will have given you a steady, disciplined upbringing that won't have suited you much. Hopefully the relationship has improved now. 1990 rating: warm and loving.

A **Capricorn child** may seem a little slow developing to you. Let him move at his own pace. 1990 rating: some good links, but there's an underlying resentment.

A **Capricorn boy-friend** is straight, ambitious and a bit dull, unless you are turned on by power. He will try to control your lifestyle. 1990 rating: stuck together, aren't you?

A **Capricorn girl-friend** is as cool as yourself, to start with. But once you're turned on, this can be a successful love affair. 1990 rating: affectionate.

A **Capricorn husband** is perfect if you want a sensible, middle-of-the-road sort of partner. This is a steady, intriguing marriage. 1990 rating: there could be another person – but you mustn't give up.

A **Capricorn wife** is a serious-minded woman who wants security in love and money. At times she'll find you a bit light-weight. 1990 rating: sprightly.

A **Capricorn boss** is a workaholic. Sometimes you feel he doesn't delegate enough. 1990 rating: not a good year for a change, unless it's forced on you.

Aquarius
January 21 to February 18

Friendship Friendships mean much to Aquarians. At the same time they want to remain independent. So they are friendly with lots of people, but always slightly stand-offish – as if they are really on their own. Aquarians are good at making and keeping friends. Primarily they are interested in mental friendship – the rapport between people who share the same interests.

Sex Aquarius is one of three signs (Gemini and Virgo are the others) that are not obviously sexual. Don't worry, they can have a perfectly normal and happy love life; but they treat people as humans first, and as sexual partners only later. They are capable of great tenderness. But a passionate partner will say they don't get sufficiently involved.

Marriage Aquarians see their partners as equals – not people who must be dominated or obeyed. At the same time they're freedom-loving in outlook, so it's difficult for them to share the little things in life. They need emotional elbow-room, and hate to be owned or trapped. Aquarians are rarely the unhappy victims of marriage. If it breaks up, Aquarians are the first to go.

Aquarius (January 21 to February 18) **and You**

You're attracted to each other,
but it's a mental rapport that holds you together.

An **Aquarius friend** is the mirror image of you. There's no reason why you shouldn't get on perfectly well, almost like brother and sister. 1990 rating: good.

An **Aquarius parent** will have suited you nicely. You will have a lot in common, and people may even think you're from the same generation. 1990 rating: friendly, considering everything.

An **Aquarius child** is a chip off the old block. You'll want

28

him to achieve everything you haven't managed yourself! 1990 rating: happier than in the past.

An **Aquarius boy-friend** is looking for mental rapport, and he should find it with you. A fond, compatible sort of affair. 1990 rating: problems, but soluble.

An **Aquarius girl-friend** is good for you. Ideally you're friends as much as lovers – and a love affair can gradually turn platonic. 1990 rating: argumentative, but still sexy.

With an **Aquarius husband** you can be a madcap pair. Whether you can stand each other forever is another question! 1990 rating: constructive.

An **Aquarius wife** makes a fine mix with you. It's a bright and intelligent marriage. She'll want a job outside the home. 1990 rating: hearts a-flutter.

If you have an **Aquarius boss** you may get a reputation as a pair of like-minded risk-takers. You really can be the dynamic duo! 1990 rating: you're on the move, and may leave him behind. No tears – you'll soon forget each other.

Pisces
February 19 to March 20

Friendship Pisceans are friendly folk. They enjoy meeting new people and can quickly become dependent on new friends – for love, loyalty and, if need be, support if things go wrong. At the same time they don't like to be 'owned', and get frustrated if chums try to organise their lives too much. Piscean men relate well to women, but Piscean women are in awe of clever males.

Sex The Piscean aim in love is to achieve a wonderful, yielding rapport with their partners. They want to melt into love-making, losing their own identity. All the same, Pisceans are fussy in choosing the right partner. Because their imagination is powerful, they can see a would-be sexual partner in a rosy-coloured light, and can be terribly let down later. Sex without love does not suit the Piscean at all.

Marriage Pisceans have an ambiguous attitude towards marriage. In one way, their whole impulse is to make someone else happy and fulfilled. At the same time, they need to feel free. They should not marry someone who will be too possessive. Piscean men look for a woman who will take the lead in the marriage. Piscean women can be misused.

Pisces (February 19 to March 20) and You

You're easy-going, but you operate through your head while Pisces is all heart. Not totally compatible.

A **Pisces friend** is a charmer, but quite unreliable. You'll have to take him in hand. You can relax together, and share many common interests. 1990 rating: quietly happy.

A **Pisces parent** will have given you a warm, sensitive anchor to your life. This parent will have been too moody for your liking. 1990 rating: trouble over money.

A **Pisces child** is sensitive and vulnerable. If you remove stability from his life, he'll be unhappy. 1990 rating: lovely.

A **Pisces boy-friend** is a delightful creature, but there may be some deviousness. You will have fun in bed, if he puts all his fantasies into action! 1990 rating: a year to keep him happy.

A **Pisces girl-friend** is a bit too emotional for your liking – clinging and dependent. At her best, though, there's a wonderful rapport between you. 1990 rating: she may be interested in someone else.

A **Pisces husband** will treasure you, but whereas you love the truth, he does tell white lies. He may seem weaker the longer you stay together. 1990 rating: only five out of ten, I'm afraid.

A **Pisces wife** can be infuriating at times, because she's so vague. But she's got a heart of gold. 1990 rating: she'll be busy in the community.

From a **Pisces boss** you will receive encouragement, help and warnings. But you'll run this relationship in the end. 1990 rating: suspicions are aroused, and there may be an investigation into working practices.

Your
Birthday Message

*This book applies to everyone born between
January 21 and February 18. But here, just for you,
is a special word of hope or caution,
depending on your actual birthday in Aquarius.
Here is your own astrological message
to guide you through the year ahead.*

JANUARY

Sunday 21st: A sensible year. You'll let others take the big decisions. There's one area of real happiness in your life, though there's nothing much to show for it.

Monday 22nd: An excellent time to be laying foundations for future growth, but don't expect quick results at the moment. You have joys – and trials! – in family life.

Tuesday 23rd: A lively year, with lots of small changes in your way of life. It's a do-it-yourself year whether you like it or not. Finances are definitely improving.

Wednesday 24th: No cause for concern. Any upset in the past will gradually be forgotten, in the light of better happiness this year. Go out of your way to be helpful to relatives.

Thursday 25th: There could be an error in your favour. You could be tempted by an emotional offer which radically changes your lifestyle – but it's an unstable situation.

Friday 26th: It's a comfortable but hard-working year. A good time to be getting a new, challenging job. All this busy-ness means that you may not have time for relaxation.

Saturday 27th: There will be a return to the past in some way. A kindly year, when officials will genuinely help you. Any medical news seems hopeful and positive.

Sunday 28th: A strong-minded type may reduce you to silence. Don't be dominated like that. Good year for education, sport and clever hobbies.

Monday 29th: There could be a make-or-break phase in a love relationship. You have a special responsibility to fulfil

31

towards a child. There will be lots of fun within the family otherwise.

Tuesday 30th: A super year so long as you're determined to enjoy yourself. Money matters flow smoothly. Take proper trouble over a new project, or it might falter.

Wednesday 31st: A hunch about a financial matter will prove lucky. You may enter into partnership. Plod your way carefully through a problem – and it will go away.

FEBRUARY

Thursday 1st: If you're fancy-free, watch out for a new love. But be quick – there could be someone else involved. You will take up a new hobby, and perhaps make money out of it.

Friday 2nd: Slightly tricky time in your love life. You'll find incompatibilities rising to the surface, needing to be resolved. Your imagination may get the better of you.

Saturday 3rd: Links with relatives will be enjoyable. Social events are a success. Listen to your partner, and you can reach agreement together.

Sunday 4th: Your most active time is the second half of the year. It looks an expensive year, but hopefully you will have something special to show for it.

Monday 5th: Marvellous year for reaching agreement with others. A smiling time, with the chance of a new love in your life. Plenty of stamina, so you'll forge ahead!

Tuesday 6th: You must deal with a slippery person, so be very careful. Neighbours will be a solid support. By the end of 1990 you reach a big decision affecting your future.

Wednesday 7th: Home life is specially pleasing. You hear news of a move away from home. You will reach agreement with officials – but won't get everything you want.

Thursday 8th: A happy year, quiet but loving. A visit will work out well. There could be a new sweetheart, but there is a problem to overcome first.

Friday 9th: A straightforward year. You feel like taking things easy. Make your life simpler and more to your liking. You will be making a number of small journeys.

Saturday 10th: Rather an escapist year. There will be

someone that you don't want to associate with – not now, not ever. You will spend more than usual.

Sunday 11th: There's a question-mark over romance. You won't know where you stand. You will tackle something new at work, and enjoy it. Quite lucky in summer.

Monday 12th: Keep busy this year, as you have more energy than usual. Be strong-minded, or someone will walk all over you. Not a bad year for moving house.

Tuesday 13th: Luck seems to be on your side. You could get involved with an old friend. Someone's vanity gets in the way of common sense.

Wednesday 14th: Certainly one emotional sadness or farewell in your life, but it needn't colour the whole year. Great time for gaining a new qualification.

Thursday 15th: Broadly a satisfying year. Expect the family to be on the move. You must say goodbye to people you like. There could be an entanglement with a strong-minded lover.

Friday 16th: After a dull start to the year, you begin to brighten up. Someone with the initial B or T could play a big part in your life.

Saturday 17th: There's a nice holiday atmosphere in your life. You seem fairly lucky. There are good links with the opposite sex, but a long-standing romance could grind to a halt.

Sunday 18th: You may get into trouble, but can wriggle out of any real difficulty. There could be a change of job, and a happy surprise by the end of the year.

Your Decade
Ahead

At the start of the 1990s it's tempting to look ahead at the way the stars will broadly affect you in the decade ahead.

During most of **1991** the lucky planet Jupiter will be in Leo. Saturn moves into Aquarius. This is great for marriage, not so good for you personally. You take on new responsibilities, and may feel hard-done-by.

In **1992** Jupiter moves into Virgo, while Mars spends a long time in Cancer. You could be lucky with money, especially an inheritance, win or other lump-sum payout.

1993 sees Jupiter in Libra. You widen your horizons – by travel and stretching your mind. But you could be involved in a legal case that drags on.

The following year, **1994**, finds Jupiter in Scorpio and Saturn in Pisces. There's some real luck in your career – a tremendous new opportunity. But it may not mean a salary rise straight away. You must work hard first.

1995 finds Jupiter in its own sign of Sagittarius. You're popular, and make new friends. You could be active politically, or taking a lively role in community affairs.

The slow-moving planet Pluto moves properly into Sagittarius in **1996**, while Jupiter enters Capricorn. An average year, with nothing vivid happening. But you seem to be laying big plans for the future.

In **1997** the explosive planet Uranus enters its own sign of Aquarius, along with Jupiter. A very important year – perhaps the most important of your life. You could break out of a rut, enjoy enormous luck, or ruin everything by being careless.

Saturn spends half of **1998** in Aries, half in Taurus, with Jupiter in Pisces. Nice for improving your income – but there's a problem over accommodation.

Finally, in the last year of the millenium, **1999**, Neptune moves into the New Age sign of Aquarius. The world will be transformed, perhaps by a new religion.

Your Year
Ahead

The New Year starts with a change to your day-to-day arrangements. These may be forced on you, or you may choose them for yourself.

Although there may not be big changes in career this year, you can make several small ones at the start of 1990. In family life, too, a change occurs.

A close relationship could be in difficulties in January, but there is a chance that you will be back together again shortly. In February you could be learning something new, but perhaps a little ill. But your mood lifts in March and you become more self-confident. It's a good month to start a new business or revive a flagging one.

Love certainly enters your life with a bang, and by April you may find yourself in a love triangle. A lot has changed in a relatively short time, though May looks lazy and laid-back and June rather fussy. Your health may not be perfect, but you become more sociable and you can make some money.

July is the right time to be re-assessing your position, and making plans for the future. practical matters go well, and you seem to be busy with children. August is lucky, and there could be a sudden break of good fortune. This is an excellent time to be making deals though you could be in a romantic dither.

You will become more moody in September, and although things go well at work and there are good links with your sweetheart, you could be giving in to inner fears.

October, too, is a month of some disquiet, though nothing nasty will happen. You must be subtle at work, and may feel that your sweetheart is in a self-centred mood.

Somebody helps you in November, which cheers you up, but there remains irritation in romance even though finances are on the up and up.

But you end the year with quite a flourish, with plenty of energy and a sense of enjoyment.

January
Guide

The New Year starts with a change in your day-to-day arrangements. These may be forced on you, or you may choose them for yourself.

It seems quite an impulsive month. Other people may act in a slightly unpredictable way, which may hurt your feelings, but you are not as reliable as usual, either – and although you will be quite friendly with people, they may not quite know where they stand with you.

Although you are keen to get on with your life and plan new things to do in 1990, your mind harks back to the past, trying to find guidance there for the future ahead. But beware of wallowing in nostalgia for its own sake.

WORK. You can have several bright ideas to do with your career which will turn into success later in the year. This is your impulsive nature at work. Even if you do not run a little business of your own at present, you could well be thinking about it – even if it is only a casual kind of job.

One problem in a nine-till-five existence is that a work-mate could be a real know-all – and a bore to boot! He or she will really get on your nerves.

HOME. Domestic changes are in the air. People may be moving in and out of the household, or planning to do so later in the year. If you share a flat with others, you yourself could be thinking of making a move soon.

It's a good time to consider the purchase of your first owned home, moving from rented accommodation to your own place.

It's a busy time as far as the whole family is concerned. You will be amazed how quickly children are growing up, and must guard against being too protective towards them – sheltering them from their own life experiences.

HEALTH. You also start the year in a body-building mood, keen to strengthen your muscles and improve your overall looks. So you will be concentrating on getting fit and healthy, either going to a gym or getting a lot of outdoor exercise. Even if the weather doesn't suit, you will be quite determined to persevere as much as possible.

A lot of Aquarians, especially women, will be keen to freshen their looks and seem younger than you really are! Beware of cutting hair too short.

MONEY. You may wonder whether an investment is safe. There could be rumblings of bankruptcy, or a feeling that you could be at a losing end of an investment. In a falling market you may feel that it is better to keep the money as cash.

It's not a good month for collecting money from others. If you are owed, you will have to keep waiting. But if you owe money, creditors will be eager to put demands on you – including legal ones! So be warned!

Racing may be curtailed at this time of year, but you do well in a newspaper or magazine competition. You could develop quite a taste for this, and plan to make extra money this way.

LEISURE. This is a good month for meeting new people, and perhaps patching up an old quarrel. If you fell out with friends last year, you could start to see each other again.

You will be impatient with a partner who is more solitary than yourself. You certainly don't want to hold yourself back.

Watch out for a visiting theatre troupe that really excites you; the chance to meet someone famous, if only for a brief while; and the opportunity to travel somewhere new.

LOVE. A close relationship could be in difficulties this month. It is certainly not a good time to issue an ultimatum, or go in for emotional blackmail. You'll end up the loser.

If you are looking for someone new, there could be several people on offer, but none of them is suitable. As so often, you prefer to keep things friendly and platonic, rather than passionate but angry!

There could be some contact with an ex-sweetheart or ex-spouse. If you always felt the break-up was a mistake, there could be moves now to get back together again.

37

January
Key Dates

**Text in *italics* applies to everyone in the world.
Predictions in roman type apply to you alone.**

Monday 1st: *An energetic start to the year, but there could be a romantic surprise. People are lively in small doses.* You are hopeful for someone's future.

Tuesday 2nd: *There's a vague start to the working year. Things get mislaid, people are unpunctual.* Make allowances for someone who doesn't know better.

Wednesday 3rd: *Still a vague, disillusioned time. Things may be done behind people's backs.* Anyone wanting to impress you should take you out to dinner, then take you into bed!

Thursday 4th: *It's the start of an extravagant phase. People feel restless, looking for fun.* Friends are not much help at the moment. Someone could be late, and you don't get the encouragement you would like.

Friday 5th: *A day that's lucky for some, careless for others. Happiness will be short-lived.* Argue with people and you'll get nearer the truth. But don't be surprised if you get hurt.

Saturday 6th: *Quite a gloomy weekend, when people feel down in the dumps. They may spend too much money.* The scene looks hot 'n bothered. Someone may try to tease you.

Sunday 7th: *There could be sad headlines. People feel it's time they did something serious.* You could get in the social swim, without really trying. Goods bought at the weekend could be a disappointment.

Monday 8th: *A realistic time, when things look a bit brighter. A way will be found out of difficulties.* You get on well with people. You'll want to take charge.

Tuesday 9th: *Much more agile and lively, with plenty of fun to be had. People won't be solemn for long.* You won't know the answer to a practical problem straight away, so be patient.

Wednesday 10th: *Sadly, hopes are dashed. A day for tough negotiations, seeing things in a new light.* Aim to improve your eating habits, which have been into junk food lately.

Thursday 11th: *Still a tough time, with delays likely. Not a good time for travel.* If you're behind with payments, people will start being tough with you.

Friday 12th: *A way is found out of difficulties. There's a new sense of co-operation.* Phone friends and make a plan for the weekend. Romance warms up the evening.

Saturday 13th: *Quite a warm-hearted time, better for transport and travel. Lots of intuition in the air.* You get a useful tip. A peaceful atmosphere at home could be rudely shattered.

Sunday 14th: *A sensitive, carefree time when people don't want too much reality. A day of escapism and fantasy.* But a love affair could have a question mark against it around now.

Monday 15th: *Still an unreal time, with people getting hold of the wrong end of the stick.* A meeting about money works out for the best in the long run. Lucky colour: green.

Tuesday 16th: *The start of a warm-hearted phase when there's a nice air of jollity. Things won't be so bad.* Beware of catching an infection. You get on well with your nearest and dearest, so there should be no arguments.

Wednesday 17th: *An excellent day for meeting someone new, starting up fresh friendships, and feeling lively.* A social occasion will be good for you. You'll be lucky one day with a Premium Bond you buy today.

Thursday 18th: *Very loving and co-operative day. It's much easier to relate to people – friends and foes alike.* An easy-going day with plenty of smiles around.

Friday 19th: *A day of adjustment and compromise. People change their minds to fit in with others.* Make a snap decision and you'll regret it later. There could be trouble with a car soon, so listen for early warning signs.

Saturday 20th: *Still a friendly time, great for meeting new people and finding out happy surprises.* Relax thoroughly this evening. Your marriage has another happy day.

Sunday 21st: *Another escapist weekend when no one wants to take life too seriously. A big emphasis on sexual love.* You want to help others, but may not be up to it.

Monday 22nd: *Lucky for some, a spending spree for others. People may push their luck.* You may be able to get off work early. Eat well, avoid junk food.

Tuesday 23rd: *Still a time to chance your arm, take risks and get away with it. Plenty of sexual happiness.* Your afternoon looks lucky and prosperous. Your sweet-natured personality gets a jolt today. Someone may be nasty to you.

Wednesday 24th: *Life suits lots of people today. There's an air of success, and enjoying other people's company.* There could be a special link with radio or TV.

Thursday 25th: *Things seem happy-go-lucky, carefree and optimistic. A good day for success in business.* You could be forgotten in a plan of action by others.

Friday 26th: *Very loving day when agreement is reached and affection blossoms.* If you work in public, you could make a new friend through your job.

Saturday 27th: *A day of some surprise, with nothing quite certain. Doubts may be raised.* There may be a surprise catching you on the hop. You're lucky today around 3 pm.

Sunday 28th: *A super weekend for getting away from everything. But for some people there could be rows.* Make something special of the evening hours. Be fussy over what you eat. You don't need much, but it must be tasty and properly cooked.

Monday 29th: *Romance could be exciting for some, dangerously unsettling for others. Don't believe all you hear.* Argue with people and you'll get nearer the truth. But don't be surprised if you get hurt in the process.

Tuesday 30th: *People say one thing and mean another. They push their luck, and may not be very subtle.* If you are suffering a loss, there will be some kind of consolation.

Wednesday 31st: *A shock could catch people unawares. A day when things could go haywire.* You could feel full of flu, or a cold coming on. Be lucky with a sentimental horse.

Wise Words for January

People become who they are.
Even Beethoven became Beethoven.
Randy Newman

40

February
Guide

Education seems on your mind this February. If you are going to school or college, this is an excellent time to improve your knowledge and enjoy your studies. But even if you are not usually educationally-minded, you seem set on a learning curve.

You may be learning a new skill or hobby, or at work you could be getting used to new equipment.

Certainly this seems a friendly month, with the chance of developing one or two new friendships and improving others.

In the second half of February there may be some illness, but it won't last long and you'll soon come bouncing back.

WORK. This is very much a time when you must speak up and be noticed. If you are in a competitive job you will be overtaken by others unless you make a big effort now. This applies particularly if you are part of a sales force, or hoping for promotion.

You can be happy that there seems to be a stroke of luck coming your way. It's an excellent time if you are workless and looking for a new job. You are more than likely to get it.

There could be more travel involved, either because you are working somewhere else for a change or because you are moving from branch to branch. A number of Aquarians will be thinking about working overseas.

HOME. One or two repairs jobs will be needed around the home. One could be caused through bad weather, another through your own neglect over the years.

It seems a noisier neighbourhood than usual, and you may not sleep very well. Possibly you will have young visitors who can't keep quiet.

There are excellent links with brothers, sisters, uncles and aunts. One of these will lend a helping hand, and perhaps put some money into a venture of yours.

It's important to lock the place up securely, even if you are just popping out. There could be a sneak thief in the neighbourhood this month.

HEALTH. Apart from insomnia, there could be a small illness in the second half of February. It could be a snuffly cold, or dizzy spells. It's possible that your sense of balance will be disturbed for a while, especially if you are getting on in years.

It's possible, too, that you will develop a stiff neck or sore shoulders – probably as a result of muscular tension. A good massage would do you the world of good, and this is something that husband and wife can give each other.

MONEY. If you are still waiting for money, you may have to consider legal proceedings. This will be awkward if you have lent cash to someone close – even in the family.

If you are trying to get a pay-rise or negotiate a loan yourself, there may be awkward strings attached. Examine these carefully, as they may not matter at the moment but will do later on.

LEISURE. You will enjoy giving a party at your place this month, probably in the second week. You are certainly in a friendly mood, and will make some new pals.

New neighbours will also intrigue you, though you may not like them at first. You are good at breaking down social barriers, getting people to mix well.

Watch out for: a spiritual experience that catches you unawares; a chance to improve your knowledge on something technical; developing a passion for a new author or movie-maker; and a holiday in the sun that may be short but sweet.

LOVE. If there has been a romantic separation lately, don't give up hope. There's a chance that you'll soon be back together.

It's a month when intellect counts more than passion. In a long-standing relationship such as marriage it's the right time to talk seriously and honestly about your feelings for each other. You can put the relationship on a new footing.

If you are looking for someone new, you could find him or her in an unlikely spot. You may not be attracted at first, but fondness will develop.

42

February
Key Dates

**Text in *italics* applies to everyone in the world.
Predictions in** roman type **apply to you alone.**

Thursday 1st: *Still a restless, rebellious time when people act impulsively.* Don't neglect someone who relies on you for a spot of recreation.

Friday 2nd: *People could be caught napping, just when they thought they were safe. A day of difficult decisions.* There could be temper in the afternoon. At work there's a fresh challenge.

Saturday 3rd: *A depressing weekend for money, though there is a silver lining to the black cloud.* There could be a new understanding in the family. Be lucky with a horse beginning with B or P.

Sunday 4th: *People could say cruel things to each other. A day of hard thinking, making sensible plans for the future.* You don't know whether to kiss and make up, or carry on with the quarrel. This could produce a black mood for a while.

Monday 5th: *A more relaxed time, but only briefly. The start of a difficult week at work.* They could be brightening up your place of work soon. You can spare a bit of cash for a worthy cause.

Tuesday 6th: *Something's gotta give! There's a lot of pressure, which people may not stand up to.* A restless day when you'll hate being cooped up with the same old people! A trip somewhere on your own will give you a lovely rest.

Wednesday 7th: *Still a tense, obsessive time for some people. There's bad news in the air.* It's an oddball day – if you normally go for blondes, it's brunettes now! Great day for dyeing your own hair!

Thursday 8th: *Nasty time, heralding problems in the week ahead. People are unreliable, and legal matters prove complicated.* But don't make a decision purely on hunch; you need a few facts to back your judgment.

43

Friday 9th: *Depressing day for some people. Two terrible planetary aspects suggest bad news.* There should be a special emphasis on children. Lucky colour: red.

Saturday 10th: *The ugly scene continues. People feel bloody-minded, without much kindness in their hearts.* There may be a hard choice to make. If meeting someone out, you're in for a long wait.

Sunday 11th: *A troubled weekend for many, with financial worries, loneliness or a lack of love.* There's the chance of travel, but you must get your skids on.

Monday 12th: *People feel trapped, longing to break free. Agreements may be broken, and people act in an unpredictable way.* If you live in cloud-cuckoo land, you can't hope to have your feet on solid ground.

Tuesday 13th: *Things start to look better, but it is still a tense, no-holds-barred time.* Be snappy with anyone who tries to run you down. Run your own life instead.

Wednesday 14th: *It may be Valentine's Day, but the Venus-Saturn conjunction makes it a bit gruelling for many people.* Take a junior's advice. You will be asked to pay a bill for which you're not really responsible.

Thursday 15th: *There's a brief pause between difficult aspects. An energetic time when things can be put in motion.* There could be a pleasant social occasion in the afternoon. Your regular partner may seem a bit dull.

Friday 16th: *The end of a difficult working week, when people will be relieved to get away from problems.* But otherwise it's a loving day. You will remember the good times, and forget a recent row.

Saturday 17th: *A weird weekend, when people's imaginations run riot. Energy could be misdirected.* You'll get exasperated with someone who acts in a silly way.

Sunday 18th: *No better, though it's lovely for artistic appreciation, or being swept off your feet by a new admirer!* You have a nice pleasant day. A new cosmetic will appeal. Don't be scared of looking younger!

Monday 19th: *Suddenly the sun bursts through! The week dawns bright, with luck, success and prosperity.* Work is boring, but there are a few laughs. You aren't lucky with the gee-gees today.

Tuesday 20th: *Things continue to look good, and people will heave a sigh of relief.* A friend looks more cheerful – for mysterious reasons. Count your cash, as you could be short-changed – by mistake, of course!

Wednesday 21st: *Quite pleasant, without any great dramas. Tempers have quietened down.* You can't be a grouch all day and expect a sweetheart to play ball at night.

Thursday 22nd: *Plenty of fun, but a hard-working day when much can be achieved.* You'll leave household chores. You aren't up to a party or other social get-together. Steer clear of the booze – it will go straight to your head!

Friday 23rd: *Wonderful day to clinch a deal, join a club, have a good time with others and achieve plenty.* Lucky colour: yellow. There could be the recurrence of an old illness.

Saturday 24th: *Rather a bloody-minded day for some, when health may suffer and travel plans go awry.* You may be taking care of someone else's child.

Sunday 25th: *An energetic weekend, and the start of a happier time for many. A sensual, sexy few days ahead.* Make sure a roadhog doesn't bump into you.

Monday 26th: *Plenty of warmth and colour in people's lives, with a liking for fun, flirting and frivolity.* A fond day rather than a sexy one. Finances are getting tight.

Tuesday 27th: *A somewhat surprising day or two, but still in an enjoyable mood. Some folk may be dulled into mistakes.* Keep it up, and we'll let you back into the human race! Your attitude will please people no end.

Wednesday 28th: *A sour note creeps in. There could be some cruelty or unfeeling action, spoiling the happiness.* Make a decision on a plan that's been hanging fire for some time.

Wise Words for February

All sorts of bodily diseases
are produced by half-used minds.
George Bernard Shaw

March
Guide

Perhaps as a result of your little illness last month, you seem a little slow on the uptake at the beginning of March. You may not be as bright as usual, and find the wool being pulled over your eyes by an unscrupulous con-man.

This mood does lift from the 14th onwards, but you could still be a bit naive and innocent, especially if you are dealing in unknown territory.

There is good news from an official source. This will boost your self-confidence, and mean that you can now go ahead happily. This could be permission or thumbs-up in some way, or the promise of good things to come in the future.

WORK. This is a good month to start a new business, or revive a flagging one. You may not develop any bright new ideas, but you are excellent at putting previously thought-out ideas into action.

Gradually you will feel that you are getting on top of a difficult situation at work. If you have a disagreeable boss, for instance, you will manage to get the upper hand – or else the boss may be on the point of leaving.

One further point: it looks as though you could be mixing business with pleasure, or developing something of an office friendship out of hours.

HOME. Teenage or grown-up children could be a headache this month. They could develop a madcap idea, and need to be talked out of it.

Home life could be a little strained, particularly if you are having to manage on your own. Single-parent families will be passing through a difficult phase at present, especially if you don't know whether you're coming or going.

It's a good time for trying something new in the kitchen, and making improvements to the kitchen generally. You may be in two minds whether to do a patch-up job, or spend more on a complete renovation.

HEALTH. The little illness that developed in February could recur in March, perhaps in a slightly different form. Try to snuff out any relapse before it gets a grip on you.

You may need dental work done. It's an appropriate time to consider cosmetic dentistry, though this will take longer – and cost more – than you expect.

MONEY. There could be a big shopping trip this month, and you'll find just what you want – at the right price. But it's no good expecting someone else to go halves, or for you to get a rock-bottom bargain deal. If you push your luck too much, people may back out altogether.

You could find that you make a profit accidentally, perhaps by not being very efficient! You could, for instance, fail to convert one currency denomination into another, and find you've made a profit as a result.

Lucky numbers this month will be even, not odd.

LEISURE. You seem to have plenty of charm, and will be a success at several social gatherings. You may also be busy behind the scenes helping to run an event with others, perhaps raising money for charity.

What's more, a couple of nice invitations are coming your way – one perhaps for a wedding where you can dress up.

Links with church or chapel are warm and friendly, and you may be gradually drawn into a spiritual organisation that will mean a great deal to you in the future.

Watch out for: something new on the market that appeals to your Aquarian sense of ingeniousness; a trip over the water; a helping hand from a real pro, which improves your skills no end; and the chance to raise money in an extraordinary way.

LOVE. Romance, which has not been very lively so far this year, suddenly comes to life with a bang! If you have been shy in the past, you will pluck up courage and develop a would-be relationship into full passion.

Within an existing marriage or love affair, too, there's a lot more warmth and togetherness. If you had a serious talk together last month, it will have done you the world of good.

March
Key Dates

Text in *italics* applies to everyone in the world.
Predictions in roman type apply to you alone.

Thursday 1st: *Potentially a difficult day, with Mars and Saturn causing trouble. But there's light at the end of the tunnel.* Happy time tonight in familiar company.

Friday 2nd: *Still a difficult time, with men behaving worse than women. There could be some deception in love.* Beware of an electric shock. Be lucky with a horse with a magical link.

Saturday 3rd: *Excellent day for meeting people and enjoying group activities. There's a great sense of well-being.* Say what you want, and people will be happy to oblige.

Sunday 4th: *Marvellous weekend for travel, conversation, jokes and pleasure. People want to relax.* Be careful not to be a killjoy among children. Someone with the initial M makes you happy.

Monday 5th: *Still a happy-go-lucky mood, with people meaning well and wanting to do their best.* You should have a sentimental evening, but things may go awry.

Tuesday 6th: *There's a strong gambling mood, which is also a bit slapdash and careless. A big decision is delayed.* Aquarian ladies should dress up – then they'll be noticed.

Wednesday 7th: *The start of another difficult period in love. Money troubles could start to grow.* You will benefit with someone else's tips. Your own intuition isn't too good.

Thursday 8th: *The ending of one chapter, and the beginning of a new one – but basically quite a favourable time.* There could be a transport snag. If you borrow anything, give it back fast.

Friday 9th: *The past can be put behind, and the future beckons. A lively, intelligent time for many.* Domestic changes are actually all for the good. Lucky number: 6.

Saturday 10th: *It's a weekend when people must adapt to each other – or simply fall out. Nobody really wants to co-operate.* Get a child to spend money more wisely. If anyone is sharp-tempered, you will go off them.

Sunday 11th: *A quieter day, when people are confused. The desire to break free is overtaken by responsibility.* Someone annoys you by being too vague. You deserve a thoroughly relaxing weekend after a week of ups and downs.

Monday 12th: *A razzle-dazzle day when people feel dynamic and a bit bullying. They mean well, but the end result may not be very nice.* You can play a practical joke, and make everyone laugh.

Tuesday 13th: *A calmer time, especially in business and practical affairs. Sensible decisions will be made.* You deserve a glamorous time today, but the fun goes if it costs too much.

Wednesday 14th: *An excellent day for reaching agreements after long discussions. Things are moving ahead.* Good time to join a club or plan an evening class next month.

Thursday 15th: *Quite a settled time in business, but romance is more jumpy and unexpected.* Love won't solve every problem, but it sure helps. Let bygones be bygones.

Friday 16th: *Still a slightly restless time for people who are looking for more independence.* A lovely day for magnificent achievements – in your dreams. Reality is more humdrum!

Saturday 17th: *A sensible day when older people get the better of the bargains. A good day for family affairs.* In a row between neighbours it's better not to get involved.

Sunday 18th: *Quite a charming day, when people feel free to do what they want. A day for lazing about.* Go try and keep fit, even if you aren't used to exercise. A strict diet hasn't much chance of succeeding, so be moderate.

Monday 19th: *A lively, enterprising time when people are on the move and new possibilities are discussed.* There could be news of money soon. Lucky time: evening.

Tuesday 20th: *Still a chattering time, when people may say one thing and do another – or not do it at all.* There's a flicker of sex appeal in an elderly Aquarian's heart!

Wednesday 21st: *Another easy-going day with the accent on travel, fun and adventure.* You won't chat someone up with too much chat! Say less – and there'll be more loving!

Thursday 22nd: *Another happy-go-lucky day, with lots of affection within the family.* Be careful not to be too strict and businesslike with sensitive people, or there'll be tears.

Friday 23rd: *People feel extravagant, whether or not they've got the money! There's a note of danger, though.* You will benefit from your in-laws, even though you don't like them interfering.

Saturday 24th: *A weekend when things may change in romance. Some people are very firm-minded.* Don't let someone else decide how all your money should be spent!

Sunday 25th: *A lively, strong-minded day when people are not inclined to forgive and forget.* You will want to travel, but it may not be possible. An old-fashioned remedy will help.

Monday 26th: *There could be a sudden moment of success for some people, or a narrow squeak for others.* You'll welcome some privacy, especially if you're hatching a new romance. But people keep barging in, or ringing up.

Tuesday 27th: *Rather a vague, indeterminate day. Lies may be told, and people may not admit the truth.* Stop a youngster making trouble. You want to break out of a rut, but everyone else thinks it's a bad idea.

Wednesday 28th: *Quite pleasant, with people looking for fun. This could be a winning day for many.* A careful approach to life pays off. Take trouble over every detail, whether you're cooking or making love!

Thursday 29th: *There could be some stormy relationships, and rows within a group of people. Some get bullied!* Plan an exciting weekend ahead. Be ready to travel far for love's sake!

Friday 30th: *Another tempestuous day when the unexpected can easily occur. It needn't be unhappy, just dynamic and lively.* You have strong feelings right now – wanting to show how much you love someone. But your emotions may not be returned as warmly as you'd like.

Saturday 31st: *Another lively, jumpy time when people don't know whether they're coming or going.* Don't let one small cloud ruin an otherwise sunny outlook. Try to stay bonny and bright.

Wise Words for March

Between two evils I always pick the one
I never tried before.

Mae West

50

April
Guide

Something happens early this month that makes you realise how much has changed in a relatively short time. Perhaps your own life is moving through a dynamic phase. Perhaps you are changing your job, moving home or undergoing big family changes.

But equally likely is the possibility that someone close to you has reached a milestone in his or her life, and this is reflecting in your own life, too.

This seems a busy month when you are going to be at other people's beck and call day after day. At work, for instance, there could be a big project that is keeping you busy, and around the home other relatives may be demanding attention.

WORK. You may be tempted to take time off – on an annual holiday for instance – but it really is better to work hard now and relax later in the year. It's a wise time to be getting your head down and no day-dreaming on the job.

If you run your own business you may find that a new project of yours has been started wrongly, or that tactics are mistaken in some way. You may not have to go back to square one, but you will have to retrace your steps in some way.

HOME. This is the right month to make an important decision about a member of the family who may be asking you for help. This may be concrete practical help – asking for money in particular – or they may subtly want your advice and encouragement.

Children are good company at present, especially a grown-up son or daughter you don't see nowadays all that often. So the atmosphere within the family circle should be positive, and perhaps happier than usual.

HEALTH. Your own health is not brilliant, but equally there could be someone in the family who needs nursing.

As far as you are concerned, a problem that's been quiet

51

for a while could start playing merry hell again. It's more a discomforting problem than an out-and-out disease, and I'm not saying it's going to linger for long – but it will be noticeable while it's around.

MONEY. At some stage during this month there is good news on the financial front. You may have to pay less than you thought, and you may be able to wriggle out of a disputed bill.

That's the good news. The bad news is that there is likely to be a brand-new commitment that you must make now that will last for some time ahead. With growing children it is likely to concern their educational pocket-money, or it may be necessary to take out a larger mortgage than you really want.

At some stage this month you could be lucky in a contest, especially if you feel you have never had any luck before. You can be quite lucky in the new flat racing season, especially if you have found a new source for tips.

LEISURE. It is a good month for going to public meetings, involving yourself in a protest campaign, objecting to some local development and generally making your voice heard in the community. You may also be concerned with charity work, trying to pry cash out of other people's pockets.

Certainly you are quite sociable, and will put plenty of charm into your evening contacts. You will make a conscious effort to be nice to people you have only half-liked up till now, and generally you should be pleased that your social life is more settled than it has been recently.

LOVE. There could be some tension and area of quarrelling within your love life this month. You may feel you are being taken advantage of, or even that someone else is muscling-in on your sweetheart.

If you find yourself in a love triangle, you need to take the calm, long-term view of the relationship rather than getting into a panic straight away. If you act in a hot-headed way, you could spoil things for later on.

On the whole it's quite a sexy month, and you will find that stolen kisses are that much sweeter than the old, familiar ones!

April
Key Dates

**Text in *italics* applies to everyone in the world.
Predictions in roman type apply to you alone.**

Sunday 1st: *One or two puzzles, with no clear-cut answers. Quite a pleasant day, but there may be a mystery in romance.* You may be tempted to do something wrong – but this won't be the end of the story.

Monday 2nd: *Pleasant and lively, with the accent on social life. This could be the start of a successful week for many.* You'll need to go out this evening, if you're young and zippy.

Tuesday 3rd: *Ideal for getting together with others, reaching agreement and making joint plans.* Good links with Gemini and Leo folk. A loving evening.

Wednesday 4th: *Slightly muddled time, though people mean well on the whole. Lots of drive to achieve plenty.* One of your luckiest days as far as finance is concerned.

Thursday 5th: *An amiable day for some, a hard-working time for others. Victory could slip out of the grasp.* You lack stamina, finding it hard to finish tasks.

Friday 6th: *Ideal for travel, adventure, getting away from it all. Money could go missing.* A chance phone call will lead to greater things. An accidental meeting will also have interesting results – but perhaps not straight away.

Saturday 7th: *A turning-point for some, but mainly a happy weekend when people seem cheerful.* Make a big effort to tidy up a mess, whether it's a scruffy home or a love life in ruins!

Sunday 8th: *Some people come up against a brick wall, but for most it's a relaxed, jolly weekend.* Lucky colour is pink. In sport you could do better than ever, so it's worth a wager.

Monday 9th: *A super start to the week, with real love in the air. People want to have a good time.* A vehicle could be feeling off-colour after the winter weather! Time to get a service.

Tuesday 10th: *Very lively, quick-witted and romantic time, with the emphasis on spending money.* Some news will be delayed or kept secret. As soon as you clear up, others will mess up!

Wednesday 11th: *An intelligent day when success is likely. An easy spell for many.* Get to bed early if you want a really good cuddle! You'd like to be far away, maybe with someone else. You could take out your mood on your ever-lovin' partner.

Thursday 12th: *Still amiable and loving, though someone could be pulling the wool over your eyes.* There could be a disappointment at work – a delay rather than a real setback.

Friday 13th: *For once this date could bring some bad luck, with Mars contacting Saturn and Uranus.* A neighbour will surprise you – perhaps to your embarrassment.

Saturday 14th: *People are still slightly at odds with each other, and a difference turns into an all-out row.* A small mishap can't be helped, so ignore someone's moans and groans.

Sunday 15th: *Sunshine and showers today, with some nice news in romance and money.* Beware of catching an infection. Even a visit to the local will cheer you up. But a date is best of all.

Monday 16th: *Still some aggro in the air, but most people will comfortably be able to forget it.* Your Aquarian charm shines out bright and clear today, and you'll be liked by everyone.

Tuesday 17th: *A great time for making plans, dreaming dreams and being creative.* You lack stamina, finding it hard to finish tasks. Lucky colour: your favourite, violet.

Wednesday 18th: *Things could come to a full stop because of difficulties. A hoped-for development may be cancelled.* You feel like dropping everything and having a good time!

Thursday 19th: *Disruptions in travel, plans getting cancelled, a lot of hard thinking.* There's disagreement between you and your marriage partner. Hedge your bets, as the hot favourite could be an also-ran.

Friday 20th: *People feel under pressure, particularly to do with career. Nice for romance and the arts.* Be loving this evening. Someone complains, but you can prove them wrong.

Saturday 21st: *For some people there's a problem you can't get out of your mind.* You feel like making a complaint, but may not know how to go about it.

Sunday 22nd: *Problems have a good chance of easing away, or* *at least people feel a corner has been turned.* But there could be a pleasant surprise, too, linked with money.

Monday 23rd: *Excellent for romance or money, especially if a momentous decision has been made.* To cheer you up, a party will be a quiet success. You'll do well in a quiz or contest.

Tuesday 24th: *Some people will be acting stupidly, but most will still feel under mental pressure.* You could be at the receiving-end of a sharp temper. Perhaps there'll be arguments about what to do, where to go, who to go with.

Wednesday 25th: *Quite an explosive time, when there could be a disaster in the news.* You can make a good plan together. Be lucky with a horse beginning with H or M.

Thursday 26th: *Slightly luckier, but tempers can explode on the least pretext.* You are generous-hearted in the evening, so your sweetheart will be happy!

Friday 27th: *Every reason to remain optimistic, even though some people are a pain in the neck.* A sports event will be a bit dismal, with few people there.

Saturday 28th: *There are threats in the air, and people are a bit accident-prone.* Make allowances for someone who doesn't know better. An afternoon gamble will pay off with a win and a place. Lucky numbers: 1, 7.

Sunday 29th: *Great for sport, travel and adventure, but still not a peaceful environment.* A live-in lover could be up to no good. Bide your time, and you'll find out more.

Monday 30th: *Surprises continue. It's a good day for wriggling out of problems.* Tomorrow is ideal for a friendly family get-together. You will enjoy yourself in unfamiliar company. So relax and be happy.

Wise Words for April

One would be in less danger
From the wiles of the stranger
If one's own kin and kith
Were more fun to be with.
Ogden Nash

May
Guide

This looks quite a lazy month. You are laid-back and easy-going, not expecting too much from life and certainly not wanting to fire on all six cylinders yourself.

It is by no means an all-or-nothing time for you. You'll be a bit disgusted if there is someone close to you who is going the whole hog, so to speak, committing themselves thoroughly to a course of action where you think there are many ifs and buts.

So you are patient, tolerant, quite sympathetic to others but, as usual for an Aquarian, not prepared to throw your whole weight into life. Truth to tell, you're rather in a dream-world this May.

WORK. You may be in the boss's bad books, because of something that you have failed to do. Your work may not be up to scratch, and if you are moving anywhere fresh your new employer will be a good deal more disagreeable than you expected.

You may be asked to make a definite choice in your career, but, as I say, you want to let things ride and not be too firm-minded about anything at present.

If you work with the general public, there could be a lucky break – and much gratitude coming your way. This applies particularly if you are in the health services.

If you run your own business you will find it a hard, business-like month, but you are not prepared to make as full an effort as other people are, and as a result you may miss out on things.

HOME. Beware of pests in the house, whether it's a young pup making a mess or vermin which have recently installed themselves – especially if you have building work nearby.

Links with children continue to be good, though now I think you get on better with a teenager than a small infant. There are specially good links with Virgo and Sagittarius children.

It's quite a good month for family entertainment, but the

emphasis seems to be on education more than anything. You may be helping children through their exams, or taking something yourself, but whatever the case you are likely to have your nose in books and involving yourself in revision.

HEALTH. Not a month when it is wise to have a lot of rich, spicy food. Your stomach is a bit sensitive, especially in the second and third weeks.

If you are prone to hay-fever, this summer may be worse than usual. If you can have an injection in time, you may find that it works wonders.

If you have a slightly mysterious, chronic illness, you may be moved from one specialist to another – and none of them quite know what's the matter.

MONEY. Luck is certainly on your side, as far as money and investments in particular are concerned. You can make a quick killing on the Stock Exchange, probably as a result of a take-over bid. Watch out for a large store being bought by another group, and aerospace and electronics could also be in the news.

You could spend a lot of time – and money – looking for something which isn't quite available yet. Shopping could turn into a real chore if you're going to be very fussy about it.

LEISURE. You could have several evenings out at short notice, and half-enjoy them. Although you may be making one or two new acquaintances this month, you aren't really in a passionately sociable mood.

Because you are a cat who walks alone at present, you will enjoy a solitary pastime or hobby, especially in the arts and crafts field. You will also enjoy a holiday involving some travel, but I think you'll prefer to be in a car than an aircraft.

LOVE. Even if you are not sociable with friends, you can be devoted to a romantic relationship.

You are living a bit in fantasy-land, and perhaps hungering for someone you cannot have easily. You may be adoring from afar, and truthfully you would be happiest if you did something about it now than staying teetering on the brink.

Best links seem to be with Libra and Sagittarius.

57

May
Key Dates

**Text in *italics* applies to everyone in the world.
Predictions in roman type apply to you alone.**

Tuesday 1st: *An intriguing day when one problem gets solved and a new one arises.* There could be renewed contact with a friend made on holiday.

Wednesday 2nd: *A subtle, intuitive time when insights are likely. People may be argumentative.* You can make a good impression with someone who matters at work, too.

Thursday 3rd: *A disagreeing time, but not a disagreeable one. People are inclined to let things coast.* You want to break out of a rut, but everyone else thinks it's a bad idea.

Friday 4th: *Much brighter and on the ball, with plenty of new ideas brewing.* A cosy evening, especially if you've had a tiring day. You are lucky – but don't rush in where angels fear to tread. A little forethought will sort things out.

Saturday 5th: *A lovely weekend for lazing, strolling and not making too much effort.* A child could be fractious, causing more delay. There should be a special touch of glamour in your life. At a disco or dance, there will be someone new to admire – and hopefully get to know better.

Sunday 6th: *Still a laid-back time, with people inclined to have a good time.* A good time for Aquarian romantics. Don't judge a family by their wealth – or lack of it.

Monday 7th: *A slightly more meaningful day when something hidden comes to light.* A letter brings puzzling news. A relative isn't telling you the whole truth.

Tuesday 8th: *Still a potentially explosive time in some areas, with squabbles likely.* Something could frighten you today, though it's mostly in your own mind.

Wednesday 9th: *It looks a bright, inventive time when people are full of resourcefulness.* This is a favourable time for health. An unlikely betting tip is crazy – but tempting!

Thursday 10th: *Lively and versatile, but there could be a narrow squeak, especially in a dangerous situation.* A piece of bad news will spoil a friend's happiness, and you must show sympathy.

Friday 11th: *Broadly a nice, easy-going day, when some people could be lucky.* Tomorrow is best spent quietly on your own. Too many people will bore you.

Saturday 12th: *Very much a resourceful weekend when victory could come from nowhere.* A loving-and-giving week. If there has been ill-will, it should disappear.

Sunday 13th: *A great time for having fun. Unexpected friendships will blossom.* You will find a friend too gloomy for your liking.

Monday 14th: *Excellent for travel, fun, exploration and making the best of a bad job!* You can play a practical joke, and make everyone laugh. Pick a horse named after a famous person.

Tuesday 15th: *Still a lucky time, when a fantastic surprise could turn up.* A few headaches at work will be sorted out. Try to finish up loose ends and get things completed.

Wednesday 16th: *Slightly more settled, but people may seek freedom instead of responsibility.* It's a busy time as far as the family is concerned. You will benefit with someone else's tips. Your own intuition isn't too good.

Thursday 17th: *A good time to reach agreement and make long-term decisions. A lucky time.* An enjoyable day – but there's a note of aggression in your life.

Friday 18th: *People should enjoy themselves, but perhaps at the expense of others.* You will clash with friends over what to do.

Saturday 19th: *A day when people may seal their fate, without quite realising what they are doing.* A secret could come out into the open. You may have half-guessed, but you'll still be surprised at the details.

Sunday 20th: *Again a bright-eyed, bushy-tailed time when people are on the go.* You have lots of ambition at the moment – for yourself or someone you love.

Monday 21st: *Still lucky and sunny for many people, with no real disasters in the air.* Whatever your age, you can feel young at heart tonight. You could make a little money on a bet. Fancy a horse linked to the home.

Tuesday 22nd: *Lots of fun, with people good-humoured and* *seeking agreement.* You could be forgetful at work. A young-ster could be talking good sense.

Wednesday 23rd: *Another lovely day with plenty of good things happening. People can't help feeling romantic!* You may have another person's problem dumped on you.

Thursday 24th: *Excellent time for striving hard with a parti-cular aim in view. The luck continues.* Play a full part in local activities. An older person will seem fuddy-duddy.

Friday 25th: *Mild arguments breaking out, but they're not important. Most people should feel happy.* You may be attracted to the friend of a friend. You will benefit with someone else's tips. Your own intuition isn't too good.

Saturday 26th: *Slightly grim for some people, with a dis-appointment possible.* Be thrifty at a day-to-day level, and you'll be surprised how much you'll save.

Sunday 27th: *Nice for travel, going places, feeling a sudden rush of desire.* Be patient if you're involved in a very intense relationship; you aren't seeing it clearly at present.

Monday 28th: *Still a bonny time, with people wanting to forget their troubles. Excellent for travel.* Good week to start a new business. You feel restless, and won't feel happy in your usual circle of friends.

Tuesday 29th: *Quite sexy, but with hostilities breaking out if people get upset or jealous.* Someone younger than yourself will be a help. Children will want to join in adult activities, but you have to draw the line somewhere.

Wednesday 30th: *A blissful day or two if you have no problems. You may be living in cloud-cuckoo land.* A phone call out of the blue will set your mind buzzing with ideas.

Thursday 31st: *Quite warm-hearted but some people won't co-operate with a well-laid plan.* You can take advantage of someone's mistake, and turn it to help you. Be lucky with the colour green.

Wise Words for May

You know you're getting old
when the candles cost more than the cake.
Bob Hope

June
Guide

You start June in a pernickety mood, fussy over things you wouldn't normally bother about. Your health may not be perfect, and you just feel like picking on people, criticising their behaviour and indicating that you are not happy.

But you don't apply the same standards to yourself, and are still in a relaxed, self-indulgent mood. But by the middle of the month you do become more perfectionist in outlook, trying harder yourself, but still inclined to blame others for mistakes.

In the fourth week things do become much happier, and you enjoy a good laugh and will be able to put the past behind you.

That's when you do become more sociable, and will enjoy party-going, evenings out, and a good time had by all.

WORK. One problem arises through lack of communication. Messages may be passed on badly, instructions get garbled, and through a technical mishap there may be no communications at all for a while.

This means that relations between management and labour are not perfect, and you won't see eye to eye with business partners. Either you keep yourself to yourself, refusing to discuss matters with others, or someone else in your company is being very secretive, much to your own annoyance.

HOME. Somewhere in your domestic arrangements a compromise is going to be needed. You must accept this as a sensible balancing act, rather than seeing it as a defeat for yourself.

It's important that you make peace with a neighbour who is out of sorts at present. If a row rumbles on, it could become quite a serious split later.

There may be a problem looming with the fabric or appearance of your home. A spot of redecoration will reveal serious structural faults, which have to be put right fairly soon.

HEALTH. Although you are not feeling very becoming, you should make the most of your looks. From the middle of the month onwards you enter a period when health and beauty matter a great deal to you, and this could involve a new hairstyle, fresh clothes and perhaps something even more radical – even cosmetic surgery.

In the first week you could feel a bit peaky, and need time off to get better. Once this little illness is over, everything looks find for the rest of the month.

MONEY. Quite a stimulating month, when you are keen to know the value of everything. You are tight-fisted in the first fortnight, and quite spendthrift thereafter.

If you have rung up a lot of debts, this is the crisis month when you have to do something serious about it. One debt will have to be paid pronto, while others will have to be sorted out. They cannot simply be neglected.

It's certainly worth entering a competition – you never know, you might win! You are quite lucky at the races, especially in the third week.

LEISURE. It's an oddball start to the month, with you still in this rather solitary, creative mood. You don't want a lot of friends around, though you may still be hurt by one friend who seems to be ignoring you!

By the third week you become more restless and sociable, and you will enjoy travel, especially to other parts of the country you have not visited before. It's a good month for planning to meet friends you haven't seen for ages, or bumping into the next-door neighbours while on holiday away.

LOVE. It's not a wildly passionate month in romance, but great for developing deep, fond links. An existing marriage will strengthen as a result, and even a love affair that has been going off the boil will start to be relaxing for you.

Unfortunately you may have a partner or sweetheart who is looking for rather more action than this! If you have – especially an Aries or Leo type – you're going to have to ask them to be patient. You simply aren't in a wildly sexy mood, until you get to the fourth week when you certainly do become more passionate.

June
Key Dates

Text in *italics* applies to everyone in the world.
Predictions in roman type apply to you alone.

Friday 1st: *A grand day for reaching agreement with others. There will be smiles and handshakes.* Make the most of your looks, and you'll be rewarded! You will benefit with someone else's tips. Your own intuition isn't too good.

Saturday 2nd: *A great time to join with others – whether it's a club outing or a happy family occasion.* Memories of happy days will draw you closer to a loved one.

Sunday 3rd: *An everyday day, without any great dramas. People are trusting to luck.* Beware of a small accident caused through silly carelessness. There will soon be a change in your shopping habits.

Monday 4th: *A larky, sparky sort of day when things go well. Definitely an air of good fortune.* A lively, good-humoured day. At work, a junior will soon move ahead, which upsets you.

Tuesday 5th: *Things aren't being worked out very carefully. There could be surprises in store.* Today looks enjoyable, though the rest of the family wins the argument.

Wednesday 6th: *A lucky time for many, and there could be an unexpected winner in the Derby.* Be lucky with an outsider. A sweetheart will be loving.

Thursday 7th: *Still a day of surprises, with lots of happy encounters for people.* At work you will succeed in plans that have been carefully laid. There should be a happy link between management and workforce.

Friday 8th: *A more cautious day, good for signing legal documents and doing serious business.* There is happiness with a young child, but an older one may give trouble.

Saturday 9th: *The luck runs out for some people. Quite a sexy day for others, especially in chance encounters.* There could be a sad note this afternoon, but you get cheerful again. ⌐

Sunday 10th: *Another lucky period begins, especially if you* *are striving for success.* Someone else's animal could enter your life for a while. You have a fine ability to bargain at the moment.

Monday 11th: *A happy time in love, when you just want to live in a world of fantasy.* A summertime hobby will make big strides this week. Go shopping for materials you need.

Tuesday 12th: *A lucky day, especially if you follow your intuition. An important day in love lives everywhere.* Be lucky with a double from two different meetings.

Wednesday 13th: *Still a crucial make-or-break day for some people, but you should end up smiling.* If you have a night-time job, there will be a special bonus to make you happy.

Thursday 14th: *Basically a successful time, especially in group efforts. The tide flows in your favour.* Make plans to beautify your home. A new form of savings is good news for you.

Friday 15th: *A nice day for some, but there could be a momentary disappointment over something you were counting on.* There's a mystery in your life. Perhaps something disappears, or someone is keeping news from you.

Saturday 16th: *A slightly down-beat day when you may feel gloomy for no good reason. Things don't quite work out.* A new gadget ia clever but not very useful.

Sunday 17th: *Again a time of some discord and niggling, with nothing quite fitting together.* At the same time, you may receive a setback in another direction. You'll be busy sorting these matters out, so there's little time for relaxation.

Monday 18th: *Much better, with quarrels forgotten and a happier mood all round. There are strong, passionate feelings.* Your sweetheart could be jealous. Perhaps you're appearing to give too much love to someone else – not necessarily an adult, perhaps a child.

Tuesday 19th: *On the whole a better mood, with common sense prevailing over rash passion.* You may suffer from nerves for a while, after an emotional ordeal.

Wednesday 20th: *Still a steady time, when older people do better than younger ones. There could be some drama.* You must pay overdue bills, or there'll be real trouble.

Thursday 21st: *You may feel a milestone has been passed.*

There is good sense being talked. Don't let someone else decide how all your money should be spent!

Friday 22nd: *Nothing very special indicated, though travel seems favoured as well as a few friendly arguments!* Work now, play later. Get your head down and no day-dreaming on the job.

Saturday 23rd: *Another easy-going day when nothing is taken too seriously. There's an emphasis on romance.* In hot weather there could be trouble with the car.

Sunday 24th: *A warm-hearted, lively time when people are inclined to push their luck.* An evening out could show someone in a poor light – or you could spy a work-colleague in a surprising place.

Monday 25th: *Quite a happy time, though there's a note of bullying in the air.* A budding romance could encounter some frost! Look out for rot around the home – and get it repaired.

Tuesday 26th: *A bit rash and impulsive, but not seriously so. No very important planetary aspects today.* A slight note of danger. Be careful when crossing roads.

Wednesday 27th: *A good day for talks about financial problems, perhaps dealing with the long-term future.* It's a busy time as far as the family is concerned.

Thursday 28th: *Another reasonable day when nobody wants to make too great an effort.* Last-minute work can be avoided, if need be. Be lucky with a double.

Friday 29th: *A day when you can create surprises around you, or have a surprise sprung on you – all for the best.* A social occasion will be great fun, especially if you're on the fast and loose. There will be an interesting young person to pick up!

Saturday 30th: *Another surprising day, when you mustn't be too rash and impulsive.* You can lend a helping hand to someone with too much to do. Follow a favourite jockey.

Wise Words for June

Is sex dirty? Only if it's done right.
Woody Allen

July
Guide

You shouldn't simply let your life slip by. This is the right time of year to be re-assessing your position to date, and making plans – and resolutions – for the future.

Possibly your conscience has been active, worrying about past failures. If this simply gives you a guilt complex, you're missing the point. The main thing is to urge yourself to better actions in the future.

So for most of July you seem in a friendly mood, though you may feel that the people around you are holding you back somewhat. Either they aren't as keen to get ahead as you yourself are, or they may be trying to put a stop to your plans.

WORK. Practical matters go well this month. You may find that you get obsessed with one particular idea, and can't get it out of your mind. This is good if you are driving forward in an ambitious way, perhaps looking for new work or a fresh project to get your teeth into.

But if it means that you are concentrating on one thing to the exclusion of all others, you may be single-minded to the point of obstinacy.

HOME. Very much a month when you must keep the family entertained. You may have children home from school, distant relatives visiting, or a spouse who needs more attention than usual! So you have your hands full.

If you are going to change things in your home or garden, especially if planning permission will be needed, it is much better to discuss these problems with the neighbours. If you simply go ahead pell-mell, you will get their backs up – and their co-operation will never be forthcoming.

It's an excellent time to be helping with the education of kids – not their formal education so much as skills and pastimes. You may be teaching a youngster the rudiments of a sport, or widening his or her mind by going to cultural events.

HEALTH. The month should be healthy from your point of view, but you need to jolly other people along to prevent them falling into a depression. You must act as cheer-leader among your group of friends.

Two other points to watch for: by stubbing a toe you could create discomfort for a while, and if you have joints that tend to become dislocated you could pull an arm or leg in no time!

MONEY. Someone may be putting pressure on you to loan them some cash. It's most likely to be a younger relative who needs help in having a holiday, starting up a business or paying some penalty.

You would like to say yes, but money may be tight for you as well at this time of year. Never mind, there is the chance of a small financial windfall, especially if a hobby of yours is showing valuable results, whether you are selling produce at the garden gate or pictures at an exhibition.

LEISURE. You seem pretty sociable this month, especially in the third and fourth weeks. There will be reunions with other members of the family, and perhaps a meeting of old friends you haven't seen in ages. Even if you're not normally the clubbable type, you will enjoy a formal reunion with an old school or college.

Watch out for: a local entertainment that promises well but turns out to be a disappointment, especially if animals are concerned; a desire to improve your own mind, getting lots of books on a particular subject from the library; and a friend of a friend who appeals greatly to you, though not necessarily in a sexual way.

LOVE. You seem keener on platonic relationships than all-out sexual ones this month. Even within a marriage or love affair you want to put the emphasis on conversation and comradeship rather than bedtime passion.

At times you may find your regular partner a bit dull, and your mind – and eyes – could be turning to someone fresh on the horizon. If you're the fancy-free type, you could well be ditching one sweetheart in favour of someone new.

Best links with Leo, worst with Gemini.

July
Key Dates

Sunday 1st: *A madcap day when people do crazy things! Quite fun, but there could be a touch of danger, too.* You could lose something personal, like a glove or ticket, that's annoying rather than really inconvenient.

Monday 2nd: *A lively, quick-witted day, and quite sexy too. People should feel on the ball, ready for anything.* A lovely day in the right company.

Tuesday 3rd: *Another bright-as-a-button day, but there could be some tough negotiations as well.* Electrical equipment could go on the blink. There could be a small breakage at home.

Wednesday 4th: *Hopes are dashed, and people lose concentration. A good idea becomes fuzzy at the edges.* Try not to be tactless when dealing with superiors.

Thursday 5th: *Things could go awry, plans get spoilt, but in the end agreement can be reached.* A sensual mood will burst out, all of a sudden. You could make love at a surprising time, to say nothing of a surprising place!

Friday 6th: *Another tender, vulnerable day when people could be conned – or let themselves in for more trouble.* At work you're in a rather arrogant mood.

Saturday 7th: *A more realistic time, terrific for travel and adventure. Taking a risk will be well worthwhile.* A domestic problem can be safely put on one side.

Sunday 8th: *Another airy, free-and-easy day, but there are snags. First the sunshine, then the showers!* Friends may turn up out of nowhere. Put plenty of charm into your evening contacts. Be nice to each other!

Monday 9th: *Quite a loving time, with the emphasis on sweethearts and small children!* You will enjoy work; there's a bonus in store. Children will be a special joy.

Tuesday 10th: *There's some melancholy in the air, as though people can't have quite what they want.* Daydreams will be fun, but are still a long way from reality.

Wednesday 11th: *Anger is in the air. People may be rash, speaking out of turn, and hopes could be dashed.* Try not to feel envious of someone else's talent.

Thursday 12th: *There is a silver lining, but the clouds look awfully black! It's still a day of rows.* A face you'd sooner forget may turn up again. Make sure you're getting enough fresh fruit and veg. You need the right vitamin intake.

Friday 13th: *First the good news, then the bad news. A difficult day to do with the law, travel, education.* A neighbour lets you down. You could be in and out of other people's houses.

Saturday 14th: *Lucky for some, disappointing for others. Victory is close, but success may still be missed.* Throw your energy into family matters, but don't expect to be thanked for your efforts.

Sunday 15th: *Quite pleasant and lucky, though there could be a background worry. Not an easy time.* Any trip away from home will be fun, but tiring.

Monday 16th: *Now the luck seems to triumph over ill-luck. Disappointments fade, while hopes rise.* Hard work means aching muscles. A long soak in the bath is needed.

Tuesday 17th: *It remains a happy, positive and ambitious time when there's plenty for most people to look forward to.* An old idea comes back in a new guise – and will work this time. At a meeting you should keep quiet until the end.

Wednesday 18th: *People need to be talked out of a mood or won over with compliments. There's plenty of anger in the air.* A memory comes flooding back – in romance especially.

Thursday 19th: *Slightly mixed-up day when plans don't always work out. A gathering could be spoilt by bad behaviour.* A career problem could be on your mind. An outsider could win.

Friday 20th: *Another slightly edgy day when some people are more obstinate than ever.* With just one friend you may be self-conscious. There could be a breakage in kitchen or workshop.

Saturday 21st: *A bit better, with smiles instead of frowns. People feel lucky, but could be on a wild goose-chase.* Lucky colour: red. If looking for romance, you will get the glad eye.

Sunday 22nd: *An energetic day, but tempers could flare without warning. Good for taking sensible risks.* Your imagination gets you worried – all about nothing.

Monday 23rd: *A day when surprises could flash out of the blue, and carelessness could triumph.* Put on your best face if going to an important meeting. If you fail to collect money, you will never get it later.

Tuesday 24th: *A day of small niggles and disappointments, but nothing too serious. There's a lack of co-operation.* You enjoy the company of people who know what they want. Ditherers will drive you up the wall.

Wednesday 25th: *Surprises and upsets are likely, but on the credit side there could be extra money coming.* If you're in real doubt about your real feelings, talk it over with a friend. The evening is ideal for a breath of fresh air.

Thursday 26th: *Still a lively, unpredictable time, especially as far as finance or romance are concerned.* A dog could do some damage when you're not looking. A gamble will pay off, particularly if there's a link with your partner.

Friday 27th: *A bit calmer, with nobody wanting to rock the boat too much. There could be a disappointment.* It's tempting to waste money, when you need it to buy essentials.

Saturday 28th: *The start of a sexy weekend, with lots of warm-hearted behaviour. Great for starting a holiday!* You may meet someone you haven't seen in a while – what a change!

Sunday 29th: *Still a happy and sensitive time, when people need a change of routine, with plenty of extra stimulation.* Don't give away a secret all at once.

Monday 30th: *Great for romance and creativity, but you could be deceived by appearances. Not a realistic time.* You may run into bad traffic conditions, so be patient.

Tuesday 31st: *Not a good day for family affairs, as people seem at sixes and sevens.* In negotiations you may realise that your trump cards aren't too good, after all.

Wise Words for July

I have a new philosophy.
I'm only going to dread one day at a time.
Charles Schulz

August
Guide

This looks rather a lucky month for you. Other people will certainly think good fortune is smiling on you, though you may not experience it quite the same way yourself.

Perhaps you don't realise how lucky you are. It may be a question of looking on the bright side of things, and trying to forget the nasty elements in any situation.

It is not the month to make snap decisions. You'll only regret them later. Try to plot and plan carefully, and build on plans you have made in the past rather than constantly trying to re-invent the wheel.

WORK. This is an excellent month for making deals with people, whether you're buying or selling. Ideally you have an important new project on the stocks, and are working hard, getting all the details right.

One thing you will find, whether in business or an everyday job, is that a so-called rival is actually on your side. After a period of enmity you may now find that you can work well together.

Broadly speaking there aren't any big dramas or crises in your working life this month. With people off on holiday, there could be a pause before people really get down to work next month.

If you're waiting for exam results, I think you will be pleasantly surprised, and better still there could be an interesting job offer turning up out of the blue.

HOME. Children are a little fractious this month, and you may even feel that they are spoilt. This applies not only to your own kids but also those of others that you are looking after.

Don't neglect old friends who may be down on their luck at present. Go out of your way to invite them to a social function, or simply stay in touch by phone.

It's the kind of month when you feel like getting rid of possessions in favour of new, up-to-date models. It's a good

71

time to be buying a new car, or changing the furniture around.

HEALTH. Your physical health seems fine, but your mental health could be troubled by one or two nightmares and troubled nights. Either you need a lot more sleep than usual, or are managing on four or five hours a night.

You are never a greedy eater at the best of times, and this month you seem to be on a parsimonious diet. You'll manage on rice and vegetables and little else! Rich food, especially red meat, will not suit you.

MONEY. It's quite an extravagant time, not so much buying fripperies so much as worthwhile – but expensive – items for the home or car.

It is possible that you will get a small financial windfall – perhaps a small pools win or a lucky run at the races. There may be a lucky financial break, especially if you've had shares in a long-established company that is suddenly the subject of a takeover bid.

LEISURE. It's one of those times when you can be sociable without making a real effort. You may have extra mouths to feed, but you'll manage it all with a song in your heart.

The platonic mood established last month does continue for a while this August. You can set up one or two interesting new friendships, especially with someone of your own sex.

Watch out for: an experimental theatre company whose work really excites you; the chance to visit an unexplored part of your country; and perhaps something impulsive and adventurous that makes you feel really young again!

LOVE. I feel that you could be in quite a romantic dither this month. Perhaps you are halfway out of one relationship and into a new one, without knowing whether to go the whole hog.

Perhaps, too, you are being egged on to enter a rave-up mood, when you aren't quite in the mood for it.

If you are in some kind of love triangle, you will have a difficult job trying to keep quiet about it. You may want to confess to someone, or stir things up a bit. The tension may be telling!

August
Key Dates

Wednesday 1st: *Excellent day for resolving problems in love. Money matters can also be sorted out.* It's hard to get money out of debtors.

Thursday 2nd: *Still a calm, subtle time, with a big emphasis on art, culture and beauty.* Try to keep a sweetheart happy, even if it means extra trouble.

Friday 3rd: *A clever day when unexpected answers are found. Not a time to hang back – better to press forward.* At work there's a tense situation. With money you're a bit of a fool.

Saturday 4th: *A bloody-minded weekend for some, with frustration and tempers flying.* You are quite psychic at the moment, and will pick up strange feelings.

Sunday 5th: *A muddled weekend, with imagination running high, and people getting things out of proportion.* Possibly you will be greedy at the weekend, so try to be on your best behaviour.

Monday 6th: *Still an obstinate time when there could be an explosion of rage. Definitely a down day for many.* You hate to be bullied by someone who's meant to be loving you.

Tuesday 7th: *People are still at odds with each other, and plans may backfire or be cancelled.* Start the evening in a decidedly loving way. You could be remarkably lucky today, especially if you are not an expert.

Wednesday 8th: *A happier time for many people, with a touch of romance in the air. Harsh words will soon be forgotten.* Today should bring something special into your life. Be lucky with a firm favourite.

Thursday 9th: *Fairly pleasant, but some people may be depressed and others feel they are getting a raw deal.* Don't allow other people to dictate how you spend your leisure hours.

Friday 10th: *People are coming to terms with their situation.*

Not a wildly happy time. At work you must fill in for someone else. Marriage, too, could be a problem at the moment; it's easy to irritate each other.

Saturday 11th: *An active weekend when plenty gets done. People feel dynamic and competitive.* Don't be too hard on someone who's doing his best. There could be problems over tax.

Sunday 12th: *A great time for starting something new, but there is a danger of blowing a fuse.* You hear some juicy gossip.

Monday 13th: *A blissfully lucky time for some, with a chance of a real surprise out of the blue.* Someone smashing isn't quite as nice as you think at first sight.

Tuesday 14th: *Quite a hard-working time and plenty can be achieved. People feel lucky and confident.* This seems a key day in your working week, when a promise becomes a fact.

Wednesday 15th: *A slightly edgy day when everything goes fine until...* You are irritated with someone who is trying to take advantage of you. You must look after yourself, as promised help may not arrive.

Thursday 16th: *An enjoyable time when work goes well and people feel like taking a small risk.* Good time for handling money. A horse that did badly last time out can romp home.

Friday 17th: *A wise day when sensible decisions are reached and people exercise good judgment.* You must take the right steps to help yourself – other people can't help at the moment.

Saturday 18th: *Basically a happy weekend, though people's affections are changing.* If you have a form to fill in, you'll flummoxed! Otherwise it is a placid day when you feel close to someone. The evening is lively.

Sunday 19th: *An excellent time to achieve plenty, perhaps on the spur of the moment.* There could be a kiss-and-make-up scene this weekend. But you're pleased with a child.

Monday 20th: *Some people are caught napping by a sudden turn of events. Others are slow on the uptake.* A secret could come out into the open. You may have half-guessed, but you'll still be surprised at the details.

Tuesday 21st: *Still a deceiving time when things are not quite*

74

what they seem. People talk their way out of difficulties. A routine job can be made interesting.

Wednesday 22nd: *A day when effort will pay off. There could be commercial complications, though.* You can avoid a difficulty with neighbours by acting fast.

Thursday 23rd: *Not a bright day. People want to take time off and enjoy themselves.* New clothes will cheer you up. Good news to do with a possible inheritance.

Friday 24th: *Quite an air of luck, though it may all come to nothing. People may be at cross-purposes.* You take special pleasure in someone's company.

Saturday 25th: *Much the same – lovely for lazing around doing nothing, awkward if you have to work hard.* You won't be happy with a sudden change of plan.

Sunday 26th: *A blissful time for many people when feelings become strong and passionate.* For once, children needn't come first. A new hair style will help Aquarian girls get their confidence back.

Monday 27th: *Slightly more awkward day, but still pleasant enough. Someone may say no to a treasured plan.* If learning something new, you will soon make progress. A good friend is going his or her own way.

Tuesday 28th: *Quite pleasant without being special. It's the start of a lucky period lasting until the weekend.* There will be cross words, which can be laughed off.

Wednesday 29th: *Very lucky day when you use intuition rather than logic. A group of people may prove obstinate.* A career problem could be on your mind.

Thursday 30th: *An inventive day when you can find a surprise solution to an awkward problem.* Equipment will be useless if you can't get the spare parts.

Friday 31st: *Still lucky, still fortunate – and a chance encounter may lead to plenty of pleasure.* It may be difficult to contact a loved one, but you must try.

Wise Words for August

To be a hero, one must give an order to oneself.
Simone Weil

75

September
Guide

So far this year you have been confident and self-assertive, but at some stage during September you could enter a moody phase when you surrender to inner fears. Perhaps any nightmares that you were having earlier are now going to be borne out in fact, or perhaps you were simply worried about some aspect of your life that you feel you cannot control.

Side by side with this inner uncertainty is a risk-taking attitude as far as practical affairs are concerned. This means that, especially from the third week onwards, you are quite impulsive, which will prove a good idea in business and romance but may prove a problem as far as family affairs are concerned.

WORK. This is certainly a powerful day as far as your career is concerned. If you have been workless during the summer a job is likely to turn up this September. It may not seem to be exactly what you want at first, but you will find that it is a surprisingly amenable job.

If you run your own business, you will still be in a perfectionist mood, not wanting others to make mistakes. If they do, you'll get very churned up, and your blood pressure shoots up!

In an everyday job, on the other hand, you may be irritated by a boss or supervisor who is a stickler for facts, details, etc. You want to do the job in your own way, or not at all.

HOME. Education is much on your mind – that of the children in the household as well as your own. There may be more books around the place, people may be going to new school or colleges, and you are very keen to expand your own mind and have an intellectual atmosphere around the place.

It seems a month full of curiosity about your neighbourhood. There may be new neighbours moving in, or you, of course, may be on the move yourself – to a new home or new locality.

HEALTH. If you have been seriously ill for some time, this is the appropriate month for taking drastic action. This could involve surgery, a new treatment altogether, or switching to a different medical adviser.

Although you may put off this decision for a while, in the end it will be forced on you – and prove wise and helpful.

Certainly if you have been feeling poorly in any area, you are likely to be making a swift recovery this month.

MONEY. You could be short of cash early in the month, thanks to over-expenditure earlier in the summer and one or two extra-large bills turning up – one quite unexpectedly.

This could be one small shock to do with finances. Another could be the withdrawal of a service in some way. You may have exceeded your credit card limit or a bank or building society may withdraw a service you've been using.

Despite the shortage of funds, you are still in an acquisitive mood, especially for new gadgets and clothes.

LEISURE. It's a good month for starting to enjoy something entirely new. This could be linked to education, and involve evening classes or a correspondence course.

An overseas holiday is on your mind, probably for something planned later in the year or early in 1991. Again this may involve extra funds, but at least you'll enjoy it.

Watch out for: the chance to travel with friends to a special occasion; a new gadget that makes your heart tingle with satisfaction; and a charitable function that manages to mix business with pleasure.

LOVE. There are good links with your sweetheart, especially someone you've been going out with for a relatively short time.

Having said that, there could still be some kind of blocked romance. If you're young, there could be objections from one of the families involved, or there may be a practical difficulty preventing you from seeing each other so much.

Within a steady marriage there is the tendency for you to take your partner too much for granted, especially where love-making is concerned. You still aren't in a wildly sexy mood, though things do tend to hot-up from the third week onwards.

September
Key Dates

**Text in *italics* applies to everyone in the world.
Predictions in roman type apply to you alone.**

Saturday 1st: *Quite an amiable day with good feelings being reinforced by love and affection from others.* Don't worry about being embarrassed in public; you'll do fine.

Sunday 2nd: *Quite a sexy time, excellent for existing relationships as well as brand-new ones.* You hear the inside story, which explains a lot. There could be a mix-up over money, but it all gets sorted out.

Monday 3rd: *Something could come out of the closet which had been hidden for a long time.* Good week for travel and holidays. Good week to enter a competition, especially today.

Tuesday 4th: *A splendid day for insight and intuition, artistic creativity and patching up an emotional problem.* An evening out will be fun – up to a point.

Wednesday 5th: *A day of quiet, steady progress in commerce, business and practical matters.* If you've been working hard, you should soon enjoy a triumph.

Thursday 6th: *In the midst of practical activity there could be a flash of subtle awareness – almost a spiritual insight.* Aquarian women may find their menfolk too weak at the moment, and lose respect for them.

Friday 7th: *The end of a good working week when plenty has been achieved and there is more to look forward to.* Good time to rearrange things at home. Quite lucky in the afternoon, especially if you've given the matter some thought.

Saturday 8th: *Very creative and lively, with people restless and on the move.* You can help to keep something open, or a local service running. A busy day with good news.

Sunday 9th: *Lots of energy around, with people being active in sports, recreation and romance.* What seemed like a bad problem a few weeks ago will be quite simple now.

Monday 10th: *One or two financial headaches, but people have the energy to do something about them.* A good day to plan your finances carefully, and make commitments for the future.

Tuesday 11th: *A reassuring time when things settle down and people do the right thing.* Don't expect a committee or meeting to share your point of view.

Wednesday 12th: *Still a sensible, reassuring time. Lots of plans will be made full of hope, idealism and ambition.* You feel nice and sexy, and will spread a little happiness today.

Thursday 13th: *People should feel pretty good about life. Group activities are favoured.* One of those days when you want to eat, drink and be merry. Don't give away a secret all at once.

Friday 14th: *Slightly edgy, manic day when people behave rashly, not always with the best of motives.* Quite lucky in the afternoon, especially if you've given the matter some thought.

Saturday 15th: *Quite an explosive time, but in a harmonious way! Great weekend for a surprise party.* There could be one moment of alarm to do with children.

Sunday 16th: *An easy-going time when everyone gets on well with neighbours, friends and family.* Your evenings will be particularly full, provided the weather doesn't keep you in.

Monday 17th: *A sweet-natured day when romance is strongly favoured. There's a great air of sympathy.* A pleasant, fairly uneventful day. You could be lucky in a contest, especially if you haven't tried before.

Tuesday 18th: *Plenty of energy, but it may come out in a skew-whiff way. Something comes to an end.* Don't make a decision that isn't urgent – new facts will probably make you change your mind.

Wednesday 19th: *Broadly a good-humoured time, and very lucky for some people.* At work you will reach agreement after a period of bickering. Pass on your experience to others.

Thursday 20th: *The strong possibility of victory continues. There's a successful conclusion.* Life focuses on home. You may get fed up with your surroundings, family, neighbours.

Friday 21st: *There's charm to ease away romantic problems, but not in practical affairs.* Pay a lot of attention to the opposite sex, as you've bags of subtle sexual charisma at the moment.

Saturday 22nd: *Another happy day where people feel comfortable in the bosom of the family.* If there's a quarrel, it will end happily. Saturday is lucky in a competition.

Sunday 23rd: *Another comfortable, relaxed day when older people get the benefit of the doubt.* There could be happy family news centring on a young child.

Monday 24th: *Not a troubling time, though a deep-seated problem could explode into action.* Make sure some paper money is safe, and that nobody knows where it is.

Tuesday 25th: *Friendly and merry-making day when people want to let off steam after a period of worry.* Lucky colour: red. Your bedtime partner will be much more loving.

Wednesday 26th: *Things go well. Easy to get on with new colleagues or acquaintances.* Nice day if you're performing anywhere in public. An old wound could start to hurt again.

Thursday 27th: *Excellent time for co-operation and teamwork of all kinds. This should be a sweet, loving day.* There is a surprise at work. A gamble will pay off, particularly if there's a link with your family.

Friday 28th: *Excelent day for partnerships and business links, with agreement likely and affection all round.* A daily chore will be made easier. A competitive day when you really want to win. Don't be fobbed off with second-best.

Saturday 29th: *A more disruptive weekend, though responsibility will get the better of rebelliousness.* Keep an eye on a child who may be up to no good.

Sunday 30th: *Plans could be disrupted. People feel that they must do something different.* If you're young and fancy-free, your eye will be caught by someone new. Don't be afraid to jump right in at the deep end.

Wise Words for September

Nostalgia is like a grammar lesson.
You find the present tense and the past perfect.

Anon

October
Guide

This could be a month of some disquiet, even though nothing very nasty will happen. In some ways you are feeling in quite a mischievous mood, wanting to stir people up and get them moving. But in another you are still in a slightly tender, vulnerable frame of mind, a bit fearful of what they are going to do to you.

Certainly it is not a month when you should dry up and say nothing. It seems a talkative time, and you should certainly try your best to persuade people to your point of view.

You may be urged to do something you don't want to tackle. This is something you can't put off any longer, especially if it has to do with your own health.

WORK. It's definitely a time when it pays to be subtle. You may have to play the power game in the office, pitting one person against the other. Office politics will be involved.

You can expect a clash of views, especially in the second week. You seem anxious one moment, relieved the next. So the argument will probably turn in your favour.

Beware of someone misleading you deliberately, just to make a fool of you. I'm not saying that this could be totally avoided, but you can anticipate it.

HOME. Broadly this is an enjoyable time, especially at the weekends. You may be in touch with grown-up sons and daughters who have moved away, and it certainly seems a month for family reunions, warmth on the telephone, and perhaps even a special family celebration.

If there is a birth in the family circle, you will be delighted with the result. But while one child may be giving a great deal of happiness, another could be up to all manner of tricks. This applies particularly if he or she is in the young teenage years.

You will have to be patient with an elderly relative or neighbour who may be taking you too much for granted.

HEALTH. For some Aquarians this could be a major

turning-point as far as your health is concerned. If you have been waiting a long time for a tricky operation, transplant or anything major like that, it may well be taking place around this time – with beneficial results.

You may be pressurised to take part in a health scheme that's new on the market. This could involve private insurance, a new form of treatment or someone new in your locality. Expect to be pressurised into saying 'yes', when you want to say 'no'.

MONEY. One thing to cheer you up is that there could be an important bargain going cheap. This could be second-hands goods that are just what you're looking for, or a closing-down sale with goods at bargain prices.

Even though cash is tight, you are still in a somewhat extravagant mood. If you have no cash of your own to spend, you will try to latch on to someone else who has! So Aquarian women will be looking out for sugar-daddies!

LEISURE. It's a terrific month for co-operation among friends. You may be working hard, but you'll be playing hard, too. You are out to give yourself a good time, and to please others. You can give a party in the second weekend of October, and in the fourth week you may well be mixing business with pleasure – for your own benefit as well as everyone else's.

Watch out for: a short trip that does you the world of good; a chance to re-plant your garden in places where it's got boring or over-crowded; and a new cultural enthusiasm that makes you meet new people and perhaps go to a special function.

LOVE. You may feel that your sweetheart, whether marriage partner or lover, is in a rather greedy, self-centred mood.

When you are in your tender, vulnerable mood you'll be looking for a lot of emotional re-assurance, and unless you get it you will feel quite lovelorn.

If you are pining for someone who left your life some time ago, there will be a chance this October to meet again. But whether it leads to a true reunion depends as much on the other person as it does on yourself. I think you'll end up in two minds about this.

October
Key Dates

Text in *italics* applies to everyone in the world.
Predictions in roman type apply to you alone.

Monday 1st: *A lucky start to the month, with the tide flowing in the right direction.* Too much to eat and drink, in the last few weeks, will be noticeable now in your looks.

Tuesday 2nd: *Still a fortunate time, great for starting new projects, travelling and getting in touch.* A slightly forgetful day. Even if you're bright as a button, another person could be unpunctual.

Wednesday 3rd: *Good fortune smiles on money, or there's the feeling that luck is just round the corner.* Try to jazz up a family gathering. An overseas holiday is on your mind. Whatever your heart says, your head will keep your plans practical.

Thursday 4th: *A wonderful day for romantic love, family affection and feeling a happy part of a larger group.* You could be on the brink of losing something – but the more you try, the more successful you'll be!

Friday 5th: *People are living in fantasy land – but it's quite pleasant! Still a favourable time for partnerships.* Loving and informative. You can get close to someone you love.

Saturday 6th: *An energetic, lively weekend with the accent on surprise, happiness and a successful outcome.* There will be satisfaction in getting your own back! Between husband and wife there could be ill-feeling.

Sunday 7th: *It's great to be getting on with life, rather than sitting back waiting for life to come your way.* Good time for a family chat about finance. You and your nearest and dearest will reach a good decision together.

Monday 8th: *A terrific start to the working week, especially if you are in commerce, sales, education or the law.* Business booms, if you move fast. Lucky numbers: 6, 10.

Tuesday 9th: *This should be a pleasant, happy occasion, ideal for partying and having luck.* Full of enthusiasm one moment, disinterested the next – that's your mood.

Wednesday 10th: *Still a happy-go-lucky mood, with the belief that all is for the best.* A clash of dates. One must be cancelled. You're over-possessive, worrying where everyone is. Relax, and get on with your own life.

Thursday 11th: *Very romantic and dreamy, but people are foolish over money and may want things they can't have.* You want to get away on your own, but it isn't easy. You'll be in two minds whether to keep a secret or spill the beans.

Friday 12th: *A more realistic time, and people are brought down to earth with a bump.* At work you'll benefit from a new scheme.

Saturday 13th: *Still a resolute time, but lies are being told and nothing is quite what it seems.* Good time for making love, feeling close. You enjoy an evening out with friends.

Sunday 14th: *Quite a pleasant day, though voices are raised in anger at one stage.* You'll be glad to put a decision off for a while. Time to catch up on unpaid bills.

Monday 15th: *Another lovely few days ahead, with people looking for agreement, love and smiles all round.* One expert may conflict with another, especially in a legal situation.

Tuesday 16th: *Very warm and good-humoured mood, with people looking for fun and pleasure.* Helpful influence. Lots of kindness from your nearest and dearest.

Wednesday 17th: *A slightly more serious note is struck, especially if travel plans or business is disrupted.* A good day. You'll have some marvellous discussions about world affairs.

Thursday 18th: *Still a happy time, though something could happen to disrupt the harmony of a group.* Quite a sexy time, but in a possessive way. You may be your own worst enemy.

Friday 19th: *A day of flair and verve, when luck could come out of nowhere.* A day to dig beneath the surface. You may hear some inside knowledge which will be useful – or scandalous!

Saturday 20th: *This bright, lively mood continues through the weekend. Things are lightweight, amusing.* You feel emotionally insecure for a while. You may be anxious about someone.

Sunday 21st: *People are on the move. Plans are being made, ideas canvassed – but it may all come to nothing.* People may not approve of your taste or style.

Monday 22nd: *Excellent start to the working week, with the emphasis on youth and bright ideas.* There's lots of strength in your love life. Despite quarrels, you know you love each other.

Tuesday 23rd: *Slightly edgy mood when people want to argue rather than agree. But there's still a positive atmosphere.* There could be a reunion, with lots of smiles and anecdotes.

Wednesday 24th: *Very lively and go-ahead, when life seems full of competition. People make the best of a bad job.* Your boss makes a startling suggestion, or behaves oddly.

Thursday 25th: *A pleasant time, great for seeing friends, writing letters and laying plans for the months ahead.* Keep your fingers crossed. The tide could start flowing in your favour.

Friday 26th: *People feel like taking a financial risk, but will draw back in time. Romance, too, is looking for a bit of a lark.* Highly successful end to the week. There could be an unexpected flurry of good news.

Saturday 27th: *An interesting day with an unexpected development or two.* Quite a sensitive day. You can be easily hurt by someone else's thoughtlessness.

Sunday 28th: *There could be one or two family rows, but it all ends up with titters in the end.* A happy evening – what's left of it. If there are tensions in a love relationship, they'll disappear once you get on with the evening.

Monday 29th: *The start of another lovely week when people should feel very comfortable in each other's company.* Someone makes a mistake, which gets you all churned up. Try to relax.

Tuesday 30th: *A light, bright, easy and breezy day when people feel that spring is in the air.* Pleasant day, unless you've too much to do. You could get a valuable racing tip.

Wednesday 31st: *Very much the same, with little holding people back from having a good time.* You could make a nice capital gain about this time. Nervy day.

Wise Words for October

Compromise is never anything but an ignoble truce
between the duty of a man and the terror of a coward.
Reginald Wright Kauffman

85

November
Guide

You'll be cheered up by someone trying to help you. This may come out of the blue, especially if you have been a bit lonely and out of company recently. It could be official help from a social services department, for instance, or it could be personal help from someone who may only know you slightly.

One apparent worry, which may have been building over the last few weeks, is a legal problem hovering. In point of fact, this will come to a head in November, and be quite satisfactorily sorted out. There will be no later repercussions.

In the first ten days of November you seem lively and on the ball, and the following week is particularly good for persuading people round to your point of view.

WORK. One annoyance is that paperwork will have to be done twice. This could be through a technical fault, or simply the fact that facts and figures must be changed.

There is a tendency for you to fritter your energies away without concentrating on the main job in hand. This applies particularly if you are self-employed, and inclined to be lazy.

It's an excellent month for getting extra instructions, either a refresher course or some brand new training session to do with new equipment or software in your office.

HOME. For part of November the family will be at odds with itself. There may be rows between parents and child, or between brothers and sisters.

There will be some illness within the family circle, and even if you are not directly involved yourself you may be anxious on someone else's behalf.

House and car repairs are on your mind. Although your financial situation is a bit better, you may be worried about extra liabilities coming your way.

HEALTH. It's a good month for any specialised health treatment that may be required. Dentistry in particular seems on the cards.

Illness, as I say, could be in the family circle this month, if a virus is going the rounds. You yourself may be laid low for a few days – but no more than that.

Possibly your eyesight or hearing could be adversely affected, particularly if you are at a certain age when your faculties suddenly go down a notch or two!

MONEY. Finances are on the up and up, particularly if you are in a job where your income can fluctuate wildly. If so, you could be having a very prosperous autumn.

If you feel you have been hard done by in some consumer purchase, you will get good value by complaining. Making a fuss now will get your money back, and perhaps something else.

At some stage this month you could have fun and make money at the same time. Your lucky numbers are 3 and 5, while your lucky colours are white and purple.

LEISURE. You can certainly have some good times with a gang of friends, and you may even be meeting one or two new people who could become firm favourites in the future.

Education continues to occupy your mind, but not as obsessively as earlier. If you are taking any kind of exam around this time, you will do well.

Watch out for: a formal social function which you don't think will be much fun – but is; the chance to meet someone famous or well-to-do, who can do you a favour; and a very colourful, even exotic character who crosses your path.

LOVE. In a regular love affair or marriage there are a few moments of irritation between you this November. If the relationship has been better of late, it will start deteriorating.

You can't take criticism very well at the best of times, and if your partner is nagging you all the time you'll begin to wonder whether it's all worth while.

If you are looking for someone new, on the other hand, you could well meet a possible sweetheart who makes no impression to start with – but gradually grows on you. This could be the start of quite an important affair.

November
Key Dates

Text in *italics* applies to everyone in the world.
Predictions in roman type apply to you alone.

Thursday 1st: *Another interesting, lively day with a strong accent on love and social life.* Co-operation is the keyword of the day.

Friday 2nd: *Even better – a great evening for a party or a special romantic date.* Work will be difficult. In the shops you could throw money away.

Saturday 3rd: *A terrific weekend, though some people may have to think long and hard before making up their minds.* There could be a sullen mood in a marriage.

Sunday 4th: *Another swooning day when romance is all you could wish for.* An evening when you want to have fun. You'll enjoy a mystery visit ending up, who knows where?

Monday 5th: *Plenty of fun and good fortune in the air, with people eager to have a good time.* You could have poor judgment this weekend. Watch out for a jockey and horse with the same initial.

Tuesday 6th: *A strong air of good fortune, whether in sport or business. Things just seem to fall into place.* Try to concentrate on the tasks in hand. You'll get into a dreadful muddle if you dart everywhere.

Wednesday 7th: *If things have been undecided up till now, there could be a happy conclusion to everything.* Good time to get ahead with preparations. Quite lucky and enterprising. You will make a swift recovery if you've been feeling poorly.

Thursday 8th: *A key date for some relationships, with things at a make-or-break level.* A delay turns out to be a blessing. Time to get personal finances in order.

Friday 9th: *Still a crucial time in relationships, with the emphasis broadly happy and long-lasting.* An enjoyable day among friends. Away from home you'll make some new acquaintances.

Saturday 10th: *Things that have been repressed may come out* *into the open. A testing time.* Beware of being stuck in the past. You may be putting off a decision. No harm in this, provided you'll make up your mind one day!

Sunday 11th: *Quite a crucial weekend, with some people feeling under pressure and others exerting the pressure!* You'll try to restrain someone who is dared to do something risky.

Monday 12th: *Excellent time for meetings, discussions and agreements. People need a break in the evening.* In any tense situation, your feelings could come pouring out.

Tuesday 13th: *A hard-working but successful time when detailed knowledge and hard work pays good dividends.* You may have more trouble with equipment that has already been repaired.

Wednesday 14th: *Much the same, with plenty being achieved. It's worth making a big effort.* You may mix with people who are a bit dim. You can't have things all your own way.

Thursday 15th: *A slightly more surprising time, when things that haven't been thought of start to develop.* A daydreamy time, especially as far as career is concerned. Good day for using your imagination at work.

Friday 16th: *No big problems, people want to forget their worries and have a good time again.* A day-dreamy time. An up-tight day. Either you or your companion is feeling inhibited.

Saturday 17th: *A more explosive mixture, with people quarrelling on the spur of the moment.* There's luck on your side. Use it wisely, or you'll have a run of bad luck, I fear.

Sunday 18th: *Still a quarrelsome mood in the air, but it's easier to pour oil on troubled waters.* A breakage in the house. A pet may be poorly. Intense day. Uptight but battling.

Monday 19th: *A more loving mood again, especially within the family circle. There could be financial surprises.* Don't let a friend take you for granted. Say no.

Tuesday 20th: *Money ups and downs continue, and people should be feeling positive and warm-hearted.* You could be told off by your boss. Sadly you couldn't help making the mistake.

Wednesday 21st: *A mild day with nobody pushed too much in* one direction or another. *There's a pleasant mood of co-operation*. A son or daughter could be giving problems.

Thursday 22nd: *Things become more lively and uncertain. There is a risk of taking things too hurriedly.* If you're active in politics, you run up against some problems. But you'll thrive.

Friday 23rd: *Some depression and worry, but people gain from the activities of a group helping them.* Good for sport among friends. You could suddenly start a new romance.

Saturday 24th: *A surprisingly sexy day when people want to indulge themselves. Not a puritanical time!* Something may now be out in the open which once was hidden away.

Sunday 25th: *Quite lively and interesting, but there may be a few black moods around.* A day of friendly arguments. Look for a new way of doing something familiar.

Monday 26th: *People can't leave well alone. All sorts of little problems could be coming to the surface.* Sexy and warm-hearted. Privately a love affair is very exciting.

Tuesday 27th: *The aggressive mood continues. Some people are pushing too hard, causing pain to others.* A difficult few days at work. You'll be under pressure, and may still not be well.

Wednesday 28th: *Things come to a head, with heads being knocked together. Stay out of the kitchen if you can't stand the heat!* There will be some cheering news within the family circle.

Thursday 29th: *A much happier time, with luck, happiness and good fortune breaking out of nowhere.* The house will be full of neighbours' children. The weather may not suit you.

Friday 30th: *The good mood continues, with Venus and Jupiter bringing happiness to many.* A bit of fun at work will be stopped by spoilsports. You could be lucky at the races.

Wise Words for November

Ask not what your country can do for you.
Ask what you can do for your country.
John F. Kennedy

December
Guide

It seems you end the year on quite a flourish. You have lots of energy at your disposal, especially in the run-up to Christmas. You should be pleased with your progress on several fronts, notably career and romance, and you feel you're getting somewhere.

But there is one area – perhaps health – where it doesn't seem as though you've learnt your lesson. This applies particularly if you have tried to give up a bad habit – and are now reverting. It really is very important to stick to a regime, if at all possible.

If you have been worried whether you will get the thumbs-up for some particular project, I'm sure that plans will now go through without a murmur.

WORK. It's an excellent time to be reaching a practical, long-term decision. There should be a sigh of relief within your company or department, and a feeling that your affairs are likely to expand in the New Year.

There may be some new look around your work-place. This could be re-decoration or renovation of some kind. Although you may not like it at first, it will gradually grow on you.

There could be a small set-back just before Christmas, but it will be satisfactorily sorted out – leaving the place tidy and ready for new ventures in 1991.

HOME. Don't think that you can kid youngsters. Children know more than you think, and if there is any bad blood between relatives, they will pick up the vibes and react accordingly. In particular, if your marriage is going through a difficult time, any children in the household will not be able to cope with it well.

Otherwise it's a perfectly straightforward month, with quite a lot of happiness indicated over Christmas. The generation gap mentioned in previous months will now have disappeared, and there are better relationships between old and young.

But something could happen within the neighbourhood which makes people think slightly less of you. Perhaps you have gone back on your word, or are not living up to expectations.

HEALTH. There are no serious health problems this month, but if you have given up a diet or gone back to some other bad habit you won't be feeling very pleased with yourself.

In the third week you must beware of straining a muscle that could give trouble over the festive season. Try not to lift heavy weights unnecessarily.

MONEY. This is a good month for finances. Even though you may be spending more than usual you should have more coming in. You seem to hit a winning streak – not so much in racing as in other competitions in newspapers and magazines, and perhaps even a pools win.

Lucky numbers for you are 5 and 10, while your lucky colours are cream and green.

LEISURE. Your social life is certainly interesting at the tail end of the year, and I think you may go to more parties than usual. If you give one yourself, make sure that you have an interesting mix of people – perhaps provocatively so. Your Aquarian love for honesty and classlessness means that you can put people together – and watch the fireworks!

Watch out for: a nosey-parker who seems to interfere in your life – but proves a godsend in the end; a new gadget that makes a big difference in your life in the kitchen or workshop; and a Christmas party where you meet one very attractive person.

LOVE. Whereas a steady relationship may still have its ups and downs, a brand-new romance will definitely be passionate. Quite a number of Aquarians will be in the throes of a deeply romantic friendship at present, one that may even be leading to marriage.

There seems to be an element of good luck, whatever the nature of the relationship concerned. Even a marriage will improve over the Christmas period, and if you are separated or divorced there's a chance that any reunion will go well.

There are great links with many Zodiac signs, but especially Taurus and Leo.

December
Key Dates

Text in *italics* applies to everyone in the world.
Predictions in roman type apply to you alone.

Saturday 1st: *An amusing, cheap and cheerful day when people want to enjoy themselves.* You'll go along with family wishes. Not a good time for being competitive.

Sunday 2nd: *Still pleasant and enterprising, with lots of warmth in marriage or love affair.* Quite a stirred-up time in your love life. You could discover something about your sweetheart you'd prefer not to know.

Monday 3rd: *Still a warm-hearted time with people sociable, sensual and self-indulgent. Not a fussy time.* More problems in dealing with an older person.

Tuesday 4th: *A comfortable day when people are out for what they can get. One or two people get hurt.* Excellent day. You should feel you've turned a corner.

Wednesday 5th: *A super time when good fortune shines on many people. A great time for travel.* You may plan a big expense soon. Others put their foot down, and you, surprisingly, give in. This mainly applies to business discussions.

Thursday 6th: *Still lucky, with no real hold-ups on the road to pleasure.* Good for sport among friends. You'll be surprised that someone close to you has such harsh views.

Friday 7th: *An itsy-bitsy sort of day with nothing much happening. People may count their money, and worry.* Excellent day. You feel full of beans. A lucky day.

Saturday 8th: *An amusing day when people want to try something out of the ordinary.* You will enjoy visiting friends. Cuddly day, unless your conscience says no.

Sunday 9th: *Another lively day when no one is particularly tactful, wise or cautious.* Relatives grumble, but they'll co-operate in the end. Don't take risks with electricity.

Monday 10th: *People can find their way round difficulties, which is nice for them but a bit disruptive for others.* You need some extra beauty in your life. Flowers, perhaps, or a little gift.

Tuesday 11th: *An upbeat day when people are looking to the future, not the past. Old sores will be forgotten.* You hear queer news, and will want to check it out. Otherwise happy.

Wednesday 12th: *People are bubbling with enthusiasm, which will upset anyone who is depressed.* It looks as if you're on your own – for a while, at least.

Thursday 13th: *No big worries, but it's still an indiscreet, sensual and slightly greedy time.* Good health. You'll be relieved that an illness doesn't develop.

Friday 14th: *An extravagant day, excellent for showing hospitality to others.* You'll feel pleased, great for a celebration.

Saturday 15th: *Still a warm-hearted time – great for family affairs, romantic meetings.* Some money problems. You may be rushed for figures, and have to spend time working them out.

Sunday 16th: *Slightly more depressing time, when people may fall ill just before Christmas.* Another good weekend. Use the phone to stay in touch with people.

Monday 17th: *Another harum-scarum day when people do not want to conform – they're all for a bit of diversity.* A turning-point in your love life, perhaps. A secret could come tumbling out.

Tuesday 18th: *Nice and lively, when nobody wants to be too serious or down in the mouth.* You could spend – or plan to spend – a lot of money. There could be a big social event.

Wednesday 19th: *Terrific fun provided you're prepared to let your hair down.* A heavy day at work. There's a legal problem buzzing in your head this morning. It pays to investigate.

Thursday 20th: *Another marvellous day if you're unconventional, looking for madcap fun.* You won't want anyone else taking control of your own things.

Friday 21st: *Still a strong party mood, excellent for get-togethers and social functions.* A friend will help with a domestic problem. You can bring happiness to others.

Saturday 22nd: *A lucky day for some, and an extravagant one for others.* Don't be too cocky. Keep in touch with a new-found friend. There's good luck between you.

Sunday 23rd: *Some more splendid influences, if you're the* *sensitive, spiritual type.* A nice scene could be sullied by a silly row. Don't abuse someone's hospitality by speaking your mind!

Monday 24th: *Another helter-skelter day when people are restless, on the move and searching.* Children may not know how to behave in an unusual situation.

Tuesday 25th: *Not a quiet, passive day. Excellent for parties, and everyone seems on the move.* A good friend will have some dispiriting news. A child is getting very independent. You'll try to tie him or her down, which won't be popular.

Wednesday 26th: *Still an enjoyable day, but the merry-making may catch up with people!* You're very conscious of your effect on others, for better or worse. A self-aware day.

Thursday 27th: *Excellent time for putting differences behind you. There's lots of friendship.* There could be a surprising event in your neighbourhood. Someone silly or worse is to blame.

Friday 28th: *Good for travel, having fun – but not so good if you're handling money.* Slightly melancholy. There could be sad news, not necessarily affecting your personal life.

Saturday 29th: *Still good for travel, and the romantic are living in cloud-cuckoo land!* If buying equipment, be very practical and compare prices. Good for competition.

Sunday 30th: *There could be a little mental depression for some, but most people feel it's a time for letting rip!* You'll be 'got at' by an enthusiast.

Monday 31st: *A stunning end to the year, with a Sun-Uranus conjunction making it a day of fireworks.* You want to attract someone's attention, without making it obvious!

Wise Words for December

You cannot make yourself feel something you do not feel,
but you can make yourself do right
in spite of your feelings.

Pearl S. Buck

All Futura Books are available at your bookshop or
newsagent, or can be ordered from the following address:
Futura Books, Cash Sales Department,
P.O. Box 11, Falmouth, Cornwall TR10 9EN.

Please send cheque or postal order (no currency), and
allow 60p for postage and packing for the first book
plus 25p for the second book and 15p for each additional
book ordered up to a maximum charge of £1.90 in U.K.

B.F.P.O. customers please allow 60p for
the first book, 25p for the second book plus 15p per
copy for the next 7 books, thereafter 9p per book

Overseas customers, including Eire, please allow £1.25
for postage and packing for the first book, 75p for the
second book and 28p for each subsequent title ordered.